temp-tations®

PRESENTABLE OVENWARE

by Tara™

D1275437

Publisher's Note

This book is designed to be used in your kitchen. The pages lay flat and have been sewn together for extra durability. Feel free to fold this book open on your countertop to follow along with any recipe.

MORE Hot Recipes in Cool Dishes™

– by Tara®

Tara McConnell

First paperback edition 2012

Hot Recipes in Cool Dishes™, presentable ovenware™, and Tara's Tidbits™, are trademarks of and by Tara® and temp-tations® are registered trademarks of Temp-tations, LLC. All rights reserved.

No use or depiction of any third party trade name, trademarks, service marks or logos is intended to convey endorsement or other affiliation with this book. All such third party trade name, trademarks, service marks and logos are the property of their respective owners.

MANUFACTURED IN THE USA

ISBN: 978-0-9838595-4-3

⬚ EGG & DART™

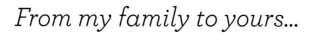

From my family to yours...

I dedicate this book to my two fathers,
who have always been there for me and have never doubted
my dreams, no matter how crazy they might be. I have had the
honor of having two fathers for most of my life; two fathers who
when together were a force to be reckoned with. They have
framed the person I am today and inspired my dreams of the
person I hope to become. As a life lesson, they have instilled
in me to always let those I love know how much they mean to
me—if not in words, in simple acts of kindness. How do I ever
say thank you to these men who loved me unconditionally?
It seems clear; thank you is never enough.

"To live in hearts we leave behind is not to die."
—THOMAS CAMPBELL

Contents

MORE HOT RECIPES IN COOL DISHES™ BY TARA®

Introduction

As you know, the temp-tations® collection has grown and taken on a life of its own the past few years, and that's all because of you! Your support from the very beginning has kindled my creativity and your very much appreciated requests have challenged those seemingly unanswerable design questions. Always with you in mind, I'm constantly happily using my imagination and passion with an aim to make your lives easier and more enjoyable. I want to thank you from the bottom of my heart for inviting me into your homes and for allowing me to be a part of all your dining celebrations.

Developing many of the new pieces in the collection has been a process of listening to what each of you have asked for in your many, many thoughtful reviews and posts. After your countless requests for a second cookbook, I wanted you to know a little bit more about me and decided to take you on a trip down my personal memory lane.

As you all know, my mom is not only my best friend but also my greatest inspiration. In large part, my love of cooking comes from merely watching her in the kitchen. She's a natural in the kitchen and has been by my side these past few years helping me select and perfect our most cherished family recipes for *More Hot Recipes in Cool Dishes™ by Tara®*. Many of these recipes have been passed down with much love for many generations.

This book has been a way of rediscovering all the things that have inspired my temp-tations® collection and have made it a part of your home as well as mine. Many years ago, as a little girl, my way of helping around the kitchen was to wash the dishes after family meals. Since those days I've always joked with my mother that she must have used each and every dish in the house. Our sink was always overflowing and guess whose job it was to wash the dishes?

As I grew older and took on more and more responsibilities around the house, I truly started to understand and appreciate that each and every minute is precious and that I would rather spend it enjoying my family than cleaning after cooking. I believe every family should be able to sit down and share a wonderful meal together, no matter how hectic their schedule. A great way to make that possible is to prepare as much ahead of time as you can. If you make food in advance and stick it in the fridge or freezer and then simply reheat it when it's time for dinner, you can take a lot of the stress away and spend more time with your loved ones. Many warm, loving meals throughout the years have brought my family closer together. From these thoughts, temp-tations® presentable ovenware™ came into existence. I wanted to create something beautiful that would go from oven to table to refrigerator to microwave to dishwasher, all in one dish. And temp-tations® does just that. It makes you want to cook!

Writing this book has been an intimate and personal journey and it reminds me that it's these traditions and precious memories that bring families and friends to the table and make your house feel like a home. Some of my earliest memories as a child growing up are of playing on our kitchen floor watching Mom move around effortlessly, smiling and teasing me at the same time. She poured love into her cooking and instilled in me the idea that people are brought closer together when they're welcomed not just to your home but also into your hearts. For as long as I can remember, my mother has always been the most patient and gracious hostess, generously leaving stomachs and hearts full. It is from her that I have learned my love of entertaining and the appreciation of our family memories and tradition that I'm so honored to share with all of you.

Thank you!

Pantry List

THIS IS A LIST OF EVERYDAY INGREDIENTS that would be good to have on hand when using this book. These are the items that pop up the most in my recipes with a good enough shelf life to purchase in advance. With these items in your cupboard and fridge, shopping for these recipes should be a breeze!

All purpose flour

Baking soda

Baking powder

Balsamic vinegar

Basil

Bay leaves

Butter or margarine

Chili powder

Chocolate chips

Cider vinegar

Cornstarch

Curry powder

Dark brown sugar

Eggs

Garlic powder

Grated Parmesan cheese

Ground cinnamon

Ground ginger

Honey

Italian seasoning

Jarred marinara sauce

Jarred minced garlic

Ketchup

Lemons

Light brown sugar

Light cream (regular whipping cream)

Mayonnaise

Milk

Nonstick cooking spray

Nutmeg

Olive oil

Onion powder

Oregano

Paprika

Pepper

Potatoes

Poultry seasoning

Refrigerated bread dough

Refrigerated puff pastry dough

Salt

Sugar

Vanilla extract

Vegetable oil

Yellow onions

temp-tations® Presentable Ovenware™

TEMP-TATIONS® PRESENTABLE OVENWARE™ WAS CREATED IN 2003 AFTER MY MOTHER AND I EMPTIED OUT ALL OF OUR KITCHEN CABINETS AND I DECIDED THAT THERE HAD TO BE A WAY TO USE FEWER DISHES TO DO THE SAME JOB. It was there that I came up with the idea of one-dish cooking. With temp-tations®, the dish you prep and mix in is the same dish you cook, serve, and store in! Not only that, but each dish nestles in a matching basket to save you cabinet or shelf space and provide exquisite organization. Personally, I prefer to leave mine out for display rather than hide its beauty, and I am proud to leave my cabinet doors open when guests walk into my kitchen while I'm preparing meals.

Quality for me has always been very important so it took some time to find the absolute perfect material for the ovenware. What I finally decided was to make each dish out of high-quality, durable ceramic that is naturally nonstick, oven safe to 500 degrees, and also dishwasher, microwave, refrigerator, and freezer safe. Essentially, the high-quality stoneware is what allows you to prep your food in your temp-tations®, cook it, serve it, freeze it, and reheat it in the same dish and then when everything is done, put it straight in the dishwasher without having to worry about it cracking, chipping, or fading. Let's face it; it is what our grandmothers used and their grandparents before that. temp-tations® presentable ovenware™ updated it to today's lifestyle.

Each piece of temp-tations® presentable ovenware™ is also handcrafted and hand painted, making it impossible for any two pieces ever to be exactly alike and making your set truly unique and one of a kind. I get my inspiration from many classic styles from around the world and try to incorporate a wide variety of colors and patterns. The temp-tations® collection is always expanding as I add new pieces, sizes, and designs to complete your set and fulfill all of your kitchen, dining, and entertaining needs. The beauty of temp-tations® is that you have the ability to mix and match because I utilize the same color palette throughout all the patterns. I love to hear how many of you are so inventive in mixing and matching so many of the patterns. Changing the look of the table is so much fun! Whether it's for the season or for different themed meals, HAVE FUN WITH IT! Consider your temp-tations® fashion that you can accessorize as often as you wish!

With this book in hand, you will be fully equipped to put your temp-tations® presentable ovenware™ to use right away! Every recipe has been specifically developed for and tested in the specific size temp-tations® dish you will need to use so there's no guessing which dish to choose. I've also included a shopping list for your convenience; you can even copy it and take it with you to the store! You'll see a pantry list, which is especially helpful for those unexpected guests, like Deana and Luna. These recipes are all simple, easy-to-follow family favorites, with everyday ingredients you most likely already have in your pantry. I hope you enjoy this cookbook as much as I've enjoyed writing it and that my family and friends' traditions may become yours!

Thank you always for welcoming me into your home.

Tara

Appetizers

PREP TIME: 10 mins

COOK TIME: 20 mins

SERVES: 6

temp·tations
PRESENTABLE OVENWARE
by Tara
4 QUART

Polenta Pizza Wheels

This recipe is quick, easy, and pretty with a delicious sauce that's fun to swirl on top. It's a great take-along potluck dish for your temp-tations® tote or to serve your family or kids anytime. Can't we all use a little "quick and easy"?

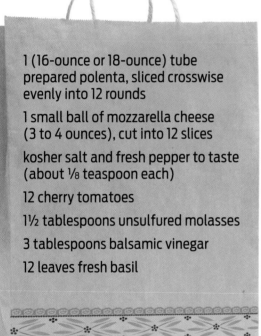

1 (16-ounce or 18-ounce) tube prepared polenta, sliced crosswise evenly into 12 rounds

1 small ball of mozzarella cheese (3 to 4 ounces), cut into 12 slices

kosher salt and fresh pepper to taste (about ⅛ teaspoon each)

12 cherry tomatoes

1½ tablespoons unsulfured molasses

3 tablespoons balsamic vinegar

12 leaves fresh basil

1. Preheat oven to 375 degrees.

2. Place polenta rounds in temp-tations® 4-quart dish. Place one slice mozzarella cheese on each round; sprinkle with salt and pepper. Top with a cherry tomato, securing with a toothpick. Bake until cheese is melted and tomatoes are softened, 15 minutes.

3. Meanwhile, in a small saucepan, bring molasses and balsamic vinegar to a boil. Simmer until very thick and syrup-like, 3 to 5 minutes. Set aside.

4. Remove polenta dish from oven and add a basil leaf to each round. Drizzle with balsamic glaze.

TARA'S TIDBITS™ *Polenta has found popularity as a gourmet food and is on the menu in many high-end restaurants. Prepared polenta can be found in supermarkets in tubes or boxes. If you'd like to add additional flavor to your Polenta Pizza Wheels, you might consider adding vegetables, beans, or any of your other favorite cheeses into the basic mixture—smoked mozzarella, if you can find it, is particularly nice.*

PREP TIME: 20 mins

COOK TIME: 30 mins

SERVES: 16–24

2 QUART

Corney Island Cheesy Shrimp Dip

We would always head to the beach in the summertime and one of my favorite memories is of Dad serving us corn on the cob drenched in butter and a plate of those perfectly golden fried shrimp. Mom and I developed this recipe for this book so you could spend a sun-filled, carefree day with us at the beach.

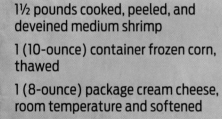

1½ pounds cooked, peeled, and deveined medium shrimp

1 (10-ounce) container frozen corn, thawed

1 (8-ounce) package cream cheese, room temperature and softened

½ cup mayonnaise

½ cup grated parmesan cheese

5 scallions, sliced thinly, about ¾ cup

1 teaspoon chili powder

¼ teaspoon cayenne pepper

1 teaspoon hot sauce

1. Preheat oven to 350 degrees.

2. In a food processor, coarsely chop half of the shrimp and transfer to a temp-tations® 2-quart dish.

3. Place remaining shrimp, corn, cream cheese, mayonnaise, parmesan cheese, half of the scallions, the chili powder, cayenne, and hot sauce in food processor; pulse to combine, 15 to 20 seconds. Add to reserved shrimp in temp-tations® dish and stir to combine. Scatter top with remaining scallions. Cover with aluminum foil (or, if your set included a temp-tations® Lid-it®, these work well), and bake 15 minutes. Uncover and continue to bake until warm, 10 to 15 minutes.

4. Serve warm with slices of toasted baguette.

TARA'S TIDBITS™ *Shrimp and corn are always a great combination at any time of year. Use frozen, fresh, or canned. You can always substitute any other seafood for shrimp, such as scallops or lobster. This dip is great for a beach party…. Enjoy!*

Crispy "Fried" Wontons

Every time I make these I think of my second father, Joe. We used to love watching games together and these were one of our favorite snacks. He'd always tease me because if he didn't watch carefully, the entire plate would disappear if he left the room for a minute—something I am not so proud of, but makes me smile anyway. Yummy!

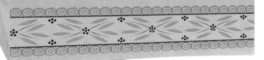

4 ounces cream cheese

½ medium jalapeño, seeded and minced (2 to 3 teaspoons, depending on heat)

1 scallion, thinly sliced (2 tablespoons)

¼ teaspoon garlic powder

½ teaspoon kosher salt

¼ teaspoon fresh ground pepper

2 ounces of pineapple in syrup (about ⅓ cup), drained, reserving 2 tablespoons of syrup

1 package wonton wrappers

2 tablespoons vegetable oil

duck sauce for serving

1. Preheat oven to 425 degrees with a temp-tations® 4-quart dish.

2. In the bowl of a food processor, pulse cream cheese, jalapeño, scallion, garlic powder, salt, and pepper until combined. Add the drained pineapple; pulse until combined and mixture resembles a coarse spread.

3. Line up 6 wontons on a cutting board. Place scant 2 teaspoons of filling in the center of each wonton. Moisten the edges of the wonton wrapper with pineapple syrup and pinch opposite ends to make a triangle shape. (You can pinch opposing ends again to make a wonton shape.)

4. Brush wontons with vegetable oil and transfer to temp-tations® 4-quart dish.

5. Bake in batches, until golden and crisp, 12 to 14 minutes, turning halfway. Serve warm with duck sauce.

TARA'S TIDBITS™ *Spicy, sour, salty, and sweet, these wontons play on all the senses. The recipe is easily doubled for entertaining. I obviously had to at least double this recipe whenever I watched a game with my second father, Joe.*

PREP TIME: 10 mins   COOK TIME: none   SERVES: 8   1 QUART

Creamy Tuscan Bean Dip

Colorful and tasty, this dip is a breeze to make and looks great surrounded by bright vegetables and mini pita chips. Remember, presentation is everything! I can still remember standing on my tippy toes and reaching into that vintage Grandma Frances fridge.

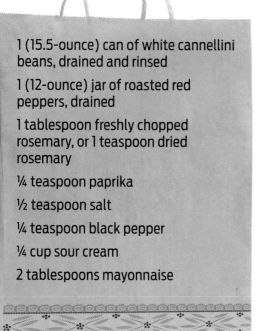

1 (15.5-ounce) can of white cannellini beans, drained and rinsed

1 (12-ounce) jar of roasted red peppers, drained

1 tablespoon freshly chopped rosemary, or 1 teaspoon dried rosemary

¼ teaspoon paprika

½ teaspoon salt

¼ teaspoon black pepper

¼ cup sour cream

2 tablespoons mayonnaise

1. Place beans, peppers, rosemary, paprika, salt, and pepper in food processor; pulse 15 seconds to combine.

2. Transfer to a temp-tations® 1-quart dish; stir in sour cream and mayo until combined.

TARA'S TIDBITS™ *This is another foolproof favorite to serve while you're entertaining guests and preparing dinner at the same time. It's a great all-year appetizer and made from ingredients you most likely already have in your pantry. You can also make this dish a day ahead. If you happen to have smoked paprika, try it in this recipe—it adds a wonderful flavor and makes a nice alternative.*

PREP TIME: 16 mins

COOK TIME: 28 mins

SERVES: 16

LID-IT®

Twisted Breadsticks

This is not rocket science, just a tasty, savory breadstick. It's an easy recipe to whip together last minute with virtually no cleanup. My family loves these breadsticks. I no longer buy any from the store. Good!

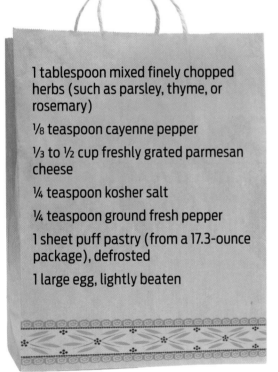

1 tablespoon mixed finely chopped herbs (such as parsley, thyme, or rosemary)

⅛ teaspoon cayenne pepper

⅓ to ½ cup freshly grated parmesan cheese

¼ teaspoon kosher salt

¼ teaspoon ground fresh pepper

1 sheet puff pastry (from a 17.3-ounce package), defrosted

1 large egg, lightly beaten

1. Preheat oven to 425 degrees. Combine herbs, cayenne, cheese, salt, and pepper in a small bowl; set aside.

2. Unroll puff pastry to a large cutting board so the folds lie vertically (the pages fold like a pamphlet). Brush dough with egg wash. Sprinkle pastry with herb-salt mixture.

3. Cut puff pastry into ⅛-inch strips. Twist each strip of pastry into a corkscrew and freeze 12 to 15 minutes. (Breadsticks can be frozen at this point up to 1 month; bake frozen in preheated 425-degree oven for 12 minutes.)

4. Transfer about 10 breadsticks to a temp-tations® Lid-it®; bake breadsticks in batches until puffed and golden, 10 to 12 minutes. Repeat with remaining breadsticks. Serve warm or at room temperature.

TARA'S TRADITIONS *The possibilities are endless for toppings when you make your own breadsticks. Our family often substitutes our favorite ingredients like any sesonal herb, grated cheese, fennel seeds, sage, or dill. We love having fun with the kids and making all kinds of shapes, like "bones" for Halloween and "hearts" for Valentine's Day. Use your imagination and have fun!*

*Mom, Bimbi, and my two dads were all dressed up and ready
to go, even before the kids, on Halloween in 1999.
They're truly what I call the young at heart.
I'm very blessed to have grown up with the most amazing
and silly people in my life. Not only have they been my
guiding light but they always made me laugh.*

PREP TIME: 10 mins   **COOK TIME: 10 mins**   **SERVES: 6**   **4 QUART**

Bet You Can't Have Just One Nacho

This popular Tex-Mex dish can be made quickly to serve as a snack or prepared with more ingredients for a full meal. These nachos are my favorite and are perfect for those nights when I just feel like staying in and renting a movie.

8 cups tortilla chips

1 tablespoon canola oil

½ medium onion, finely chopped

12 ounces lean ground beef

1 cup black beans, rinsed and drained

3 tablespoons taco seasoning

6 ounces (2 cups) shredded Mexican four-cheese mix

1 jalapeno, sliced into rounds

⅓ cup salsa

¼ cup sour cream

1. Preheat oven to 350 degrees. Place half of the tortilla chips into a 4-quart temp-tations® dish and set aside.

2. In a large skillet over medium-high, heat oil and cook onions until the onions become soft and translucent, 3 to 5 minutes.

3. Add the beef, beans, and taco seasoning. Cook, breaking up the meat with a wooden spoon, until the meat is cooked through and crumbled, about 5 minutes.

4. Top the chips with half of the beef mixture, half of the cheese, and half of the jalapenos. Repeat with the remaining chips, beef, cheese, and jalapenos.

5. Bake until heated through and the cheese is melted and bubbly, 10 minutes. Serve with salsa and a large dollop of sour cream.

TARA'S TIDBITS™ *A variation may consist of a taco shell topped with a layer of refried beans and/or some of the following common toppings: cilantro, chicken, carne asada, guacamole, lettuce, lime, olives, onions, or tomatoes. Use your favorite temp-tations® bowls or dipping dishes and let your guests create their own fiesta!*

Divine Swine & Monterey Jack Meatballs

If it oinks like a meatball, you know that it's Mom's! These meatballs were so popular when we were growing up that Mom always made sure she prepared a double batch. Not because that was the only dish she brought, served, or brought along as potluck, but because she knew two little thieves would devour at least a dozen of them before she even hit the door. The names of those two theives were Tracy and Tara.

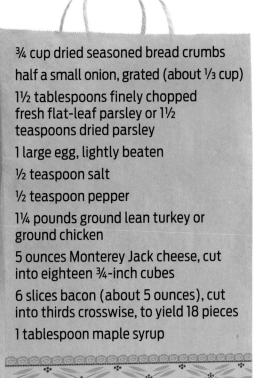

¾ cup dried seasoned bread crumbs

half a small onion, grated (about ⅓ cup)

1½ tablespoons finely chopped fresh flat-leaf parsley or 1½ teaspoons dried parsley

1 large egg, lightly beaten

½ teaspoon salt

½ teaspoon pepper

1¼ pounds ground lean turkey or ground chicken

5 ounces Monterey Jack cheese, cut into eighteen ¾-inch cubes

6 slices bacon (about 5 ounces), cut into thirds crosswise, to yield 18 pieces

1 tablespoon maple syrup

1. Preheat oven to 400 degrees. Combine bread crumbs, onion, parsley, egg, salt, and pepper in a bowl. Add ground turkey and mix thoroughly to combine.

2. With your hands, form eighteen 1½-inch meatballs around a cube of cheese. Wrap each meatball with 1 piece of bacon, tucking under the sides.

3. Place meatballs, seam side down, in 2.5-quart temp-tations® dish. Bake until meatballs are no longer pink, 25 minutes. Brush tops with maple syrup; bake until bacon is crispy, 10 minutes more.

4. Serve warm, with toothpicks.

TARA'S TIDBITS™ *I haven't forgotten you meat lovers. You can always substitute 1¼ pounds of ground beef, or ¾ pound ground beef and ½ pound ground pork, instead of the turkey or chicken in this recipe. For more spice, try Monterey Pepper Jack cheese.*

PREP TIME: 15 mins

COOK TIME: 20 mins

SERVES: 2

temp·tations
PRESENTABLE OVENWARE
by Tara

TWO 18-OUNCE SOUP BOWLS

Creamy Sausage Vegetable Soup

This easy-to-follow recipe is not only quick but it's completely made in your microwave! If you care to lighten this soup recipe, you can always substitute either chicken or turkey sausage and/or low-fat cream as well as low-sodium vegetable broth.

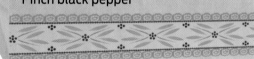

2 links sweet Italian sausage
(5 to 6 ounces)

1 (14.5-ounce) can vegetable broth

⅓ cup heavy cream

1 small red potato, cut into ½-inch
pieces

2 small carrots, peeled and thinly sliced

1 stalk celery, thinly sliced

1 small shallot or 1 small onion,
finely chopped

1 (15.5-ounce) can black-eyed peas,
drained and rinsed

¼ teaspoon salt

Pinch black pepper

1. With a fork, pierce sausage all over. Place in 1 temp-tations® bowl. Microwave 6–8 minutes, until just no longer pink. Remove sausage to a plate lined with a paper towel to drain and set aside. Wipe fat from dish with a paper towel; reserve dish.

2. Divide vegetable broth, heavy cream, and potatoes between two temp-tations® bowls and microwave until potatoes are al dente, 6 to 8 minutes.

3. Cut reserved cooked sausage into bite-size pieces and add to the two temp-tations® dishes with remaining ingredients. Microwave until vegetables are tender and soup is heated through, 8 to 10 minutes.

4. Serve with freshly baked biscuits, rolls, or toast.

TARA'S TRADITIONS *Maybe it was because I was so small, but the snowdrifts I remember as a child in upstate New York seemed just about twice my size. Just before my snowsuit was soaked through from making my hundredth snow angel, Mom always called us in for this amazing soup. Besides tasting like heaven, it warmed me up even before I could take my mittens off.*

PREP TIME: 15 mins

COOK TIME: 27 mins

SERVES: 4

LID-IT®

Puffed Pastry Caramelized Onion Tarts

One of my favorite things to make with caramelized onions is a tart. You can tell because I have another one in this book! This one is so easy and tastes incredible. The sweetness of the onions on the thin, crispy, flaky pastry base with a crumbling of feta cheese is delicious.

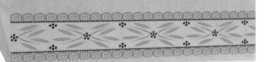

1 sheet puff pastry (from a 17.3-oz package), defrosted in refrigerator

1 tablespoon plus 1 teaspoon extra-virgin olive oil

2 small red onions (4 ounces each), peeled and sliced into ¼-inch-thick rounds (9 slices)

1 tablespoon red wine vinegar

2 teaspoons fresh oregano leaves, torn

¼ teaspoon kosher salt

⅛ teaspoon fresh ground pepper

⅓ cup crumbled feta cheese (2 ounces)

1. Preheat oven to 425 degrees. Unroll puff pastry onto a temp-tations® Lid-it®. Cut pastry into 3-inch by 3-inch squares. Make a ¼-inch border inside each square. Line up pastry squares ½ inch apart. Return to refrigerator.

2. Heat a large nonstick pan over medium-high heat with 1 tablespoon olive oil. Add onion slices and cook in one layer, in batches if necessary, until softened and brown, 4 to 5 minutes. Flip onions and cook on second side until softened, 5 minutes.

3. Remove pan from heat; add vinegar and 1 teaspoon oregano. Season with salt and pepper.

4. Place onion slice inside each square; top with feta and remaining 1 teaspoon olive oil.

5. Bake tarts until pastry is puffed and golden and onions are caramelized, 12 minutes. Garnish with remaining 1 teaspoon oregano. Serve immediately.

TARA'S TIDBITS™ *Any other herbs such as thyme or rosemary are great too. Not only are these tarts an elegant brunch, I've also served them as starters or for lunch. They are really versatile; you can use whatever cheese you like, too. Why not try smoked mozzarella and basil; or haloumi, mint, and oregano; or try red onions with goat's cheese and rosemary.*

Joey's Homemade Cheese Crackers

So easy to make, and a great natural alternative to the store-bought versions.

4 tablespoons butter, softened

1 cup shredded sharp cheddar cheese

1 cup whole wheat flour

2 tablespoons warm water

¼ teaspoon baking powder

¼ teaspoon onion powder

¼ teaspoon paprika

¼ teaspoon coarse salt

coarse salt, optional

1. Preheat oven to 350 degrees.

2. In a large mixing bowl, whisk the softened butter until smooth and then fold in shredded cheddar cheese.

3. Add all remaining ingredients except coarse salt to the bowl and knead until a thick dough is formed.

4. Lay out a long sheet of parchment paper and place dough on top of the Lid-it®, pressing down to flatten. Cover with an additional sheet of parchment paper. Use a rolling pin on top of the parchment paper to roll the dough out to a thickness of about ⅛ inch.

5. Discard top sheet of parchment paper and slice the rolled-out dough into 1-inch squares. Transfer cut squares from the parchment paper to a Lid-it®. Pierce each square with a fork and sprinkle with coarse salt, if desired.

6. Bake 15 to 20 minutes, or until golden brown. Let cool on pan before serving.

TARA'S TRADITIONS *Joey loves these homemade cheese crackers so much they rarely make it out of my kitchen. Every time he visits with his auntie Tara, we bake these together.*

This photo was taken just this past Christmas, 2011, in front of Radio City Music Hall. I took Mom, Bimbi, Jenn, and Macaylan to the Christmas Spectacular Show starring the famous Rockettes in New York City. This was Macaylan's first time at Radio City, and we were especially lucky to meet one of the Rockettes before the show. Macaylan was awestruck to meet an official Rockette in person and mesmerized by the show. It was a very special day and a treasured Christmas memory for all of us. Macaylan loved the New York hot dog we ate from the stand in front of Radio City Music Hall, and whenever we make Pigs in Blankets we wink at each other and remember our amazing day with the Rockettes.

PREP TIME: 15 mins

COOK TIME: 35 mins

SERVES: 12

LID-IT®

Macaylan's Pigs in Blankets

It's not a party without these tried-and-true classics...great for kids and adults alike. My mom used to make them all the time for us when we were young, and now I am happy to pass them down to the next generation. One thing is for sure, these are a hit anytime. It's always the first empty platter on its way back to the kitchen!

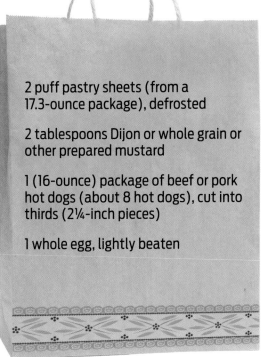

2 puff pastry sheets (from a 17.3-ounce package), defrosted

2 tablespoons Dijon or whole grain or other prepared mustard

1 (16-ounce) package of beef or pork hot dogs (about 8 hot dogs), cut into thirds (2¼-inch pieces)

1 whole egg, lightly beaten

1. Preheat oven to 425 degrees.

2. Unroll puff pastry to a large cutting board. Roll puff pastry sheet to a 10-inch by 9½-inch rectangle.

3. Cut puff pastry into 12 rectangles, measuring 2½ inches by 3¼ inches. Dollop ¼ teaspoon mustard on the center of each pastry and place cut hot dog on top of mustard. Brush one end of dough with egg and roll hot dog up, ending with egg-washed end, overlapping dough slightly. Repeat with remaining puff pastry.

4. Brush rolled-up dough with egg and transfer pastry to a temp-tations® Lid-it®. Chill in freezer 10 minutes. (Pigs in blankets can be frozen at this point up to 1 month; bake frozen in preheated 425-degree oven for 25 to 27 minutes.)

5. Bake pigs in blankets until puffed and golden, about 20 minutes. Serve warm.

TARA'S TRADITIONS *You can always choose your own condiments: mustard, ketchup, even relish—make them into one-bite treats. Less mess, more fun. I like to wrap mine in crisp bacon slices (secure them with toothpicks) and even melt cheese on top. This is how Macaylan, my goddaughter, loves them best.*

PREP TIME: 5 mins

COOK TIME: 2 hours

SERVES: 4

LID-IT®

Old-Fashioned Baked Apple Chips

These are perfect for after-school snacks or on-the-road trips.
Try experimenting with different varieties of apples.

2 large apples

2 tablespoons sugar

1 teaspoon ground cinnamon

1. Preheat oven to 215 degrees.

2. Core apples, if desired. This is not entirely necessary, as the apple will get crisp enough to eat core and all.

3. Use a mandoline or very sharp knife to cut whole apples into ⅛-inch slices. If you chose not to core the apples, shake any seeds from the slices. Arrange slices in a single layer on the Lid-it®.

4. Combine sugar and cinnamon and sprinkle over all sliced apples.

5. Bake 2 hours before turning the oven off, leaving the apples still inside. Let apples sit in the warm oven overnight.

6. Apples should be very crisp. If not, you can turn the oven back up to 200 degrees and continue baking until they are.

TARA'S TRADITIONS *My grandmother always made apple and banana chips with a dehydrator and they were amazing ... so I had to figure out how to do it my own way!*

PREP TIME: 5 mins

COOK TIME: 15 mins

SERVES: 12

LID-IT®

Glazed Pecans

So easy to make, these sweet and salty bites are crunchy and delicious! And easy to make. I mean really!

2 cups pecans

1 tablespoon honey

2 teaspoons canola oil

1 tablespoon water

¼ teaspoon ground cinnamon

1½ tablespoons sugar

½ teaspoon salt

1. Preheat oven to 325 degrees.

2. In a mixing bowl, toss together pecans, honey, canola oil, water, and cinnamon until pecans are fully coated.

3. Spread coated pecans in a single layer on the Lid-it® and bake 15 minutes, stirring halfway through.

4. Remove pecans from oven and toss in sugar and salt before serving.

TARA'S TIDBITS™ *I love these nuts on a salad, but they are delicious just about anytime and for any meal. Chop and sprinkle over ice cream, or use as a party snack!*

PREP TIME: 25 mins

COOK TIME: 30 mins

SERVES: 6

temp·tations
PRESENTABLE OVENWARE
by Tara
2.5 QUART

Stuffed Pizza Spirals

My grandma Frances always had her priorities straight. Her legendary stuffed pizza spirals first, and a change of muddy soccer clothes second. This recipe makes eighteen spirals and I watched Grandma very carefully to make sure everyone recieved the same amount.

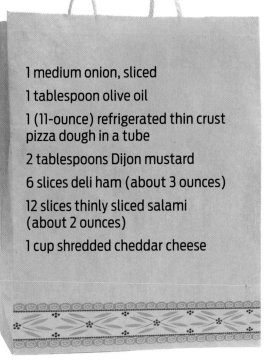

1 medium onion, sliced

1 tablespoon olive oil

1 (11-ounce) refrigerated thin crust pizza dough in a tube

2 tablespoons Dijon mustard

6 slices deli ham (about 3 ounces)

12 slices thinly sliced salami (about 2 ounces)

1 cup shredded cheddar cheese

1. Preheat oven to 425 degrees.

2. Sauté onion and olive oil in a medium pan over medium-high heat, until onions are translucent and browned, 10 to 12 minutes. Set aside to cool.

3. On a floured surface, roll pizza dough into a 10-inch by 15-inch rectangle. Layer with mustard, ham, salami, cheddar, and reserved onion. Cut dough in half lengthwise and roll each half, crosswise, into a 15-inch-long spiral. Cut each spiral into thirds, and then thirds again, to yield 18 spirals.

4. Re-roll as needed and place spirals, facing up, in a temp-tations® 2.5-quart dish, sprayed with any type of cooking spray you prefer, or have on hand.

5. Bake until golden brown, 20 minutes.

TARA'S TRADITIONS *There is nothing I would change in this recipe, or in Grandma Frances. She's always been a great source of my inspiration and a grandmother just as charming as our Old World pattern.*

PREP TIME: 20 mins

COOK TIME: 15 mins

SERVES: 4

temp·tations.
PRESENTABLE OVENWARE
by Tara

2 QUART

Mouthwatering Stuffed Mushrooms

Mom makes these every holiday and they're beyond awesome! It's my go-to stuffed mushroom recipe.

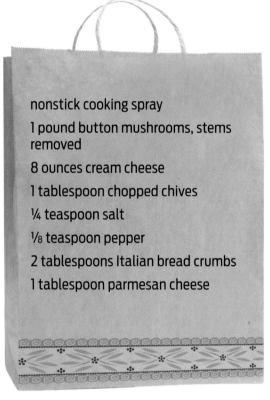

nonstick cooking spray

1 pound button mushrooms, stems removed

8 ounces cream cheese

1 tablespoon chopped chives

¼ teaspoon salt

⅛ teaspoon pepper

2 tablespoons Italian bread crumbs

1 tablespoon parmesan cheese

1. Preheat oven to 375 degrees. Spray ovenware with nonstick cooking spray and arrange mushroom caps, tops down.

2. In a food processor, pulse cream cheese, chives, salt, and pepper until well combined.

3. Fill each mushroom cap with an even amount of the cream cheese mixture.

4. Combine bread crumbs and parmesan cheese and sprinkle on top of the stuffed mushrooms.

5. Bake 12 to 15 minutes, or until mushrooms are tender and filling is hot. Serve immediately.

TARA'S TRADITIONS *Mom sometimes adds hot Italian sausage or crabmeat for variety.*

PREP TIME: 20 mins

COOK TIME: 22 mins

SERVES: 4

temp·tations
PRESENTABLE OVENWARE
by tara
4 QUART

Whistle Stop "Fried" Green Totmatoes

These are not greasy. They're tasty and much healthier!

nonstick cooking spray

4 green tomatoes

2 large egg whites

½ cup buttermilk

¼ cup water

¾ cup all-purpose flour

¼ cup cornmeal

¼ teaspoon onion powder

¼ teaspoon salt

¼ teaspoon pepper

1. Preheat oven to 400 degrees. Spray ovenware with nonstick cooking spray.

2. Slice ends off green tomatoes and discard. Slice the trimmed tomatoes into ¼-inch-thick slices.

3. In a mixing bowl, whisk together egg whites, buttermilk, and water. In a separate bowl, combine flour, cornmeal, onion powder, salt, and pepper.

4. Double-bread each tomato slice by first dipping into the egg mixture, then the flour mixture, then repeating. Place onto the greased ovenware as you go, arranging all breaded tomato slices in a single layer.

5. Bake 10 minutes, flip, and bake an additional 8 to 12 minutes, or until tomato slices are lightly browned. Serve hot.

TARA'S TIDBITS™ *They do get crispy and brown, but you have to slice them really thin. Enjoy!*

PREP TIME: 20 mins

  COOK TIME: 10 mins

SERVES: 4

 temp·tations.
PRESENTABLE OVENWARE
by Tara
LID-IT®

Jenn's Coconut Shrimp

I'm obsessed with this recipe. It's much healthier than frying but does not forfeit taste.

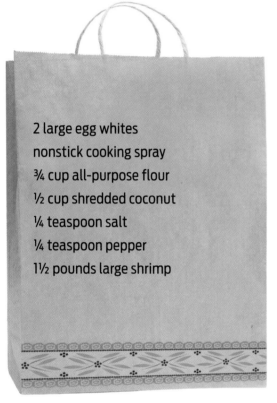

2 large egg whites

nonstick cooking spray

¾ cup all-purpose flour

½ cup shredded coconut

¼ teaspoon salt

¼ teaspoon pepper

1½ pounds large shrimp

1. Preheat oven to 500 degrees. Spray ovenware with nonstick cooking spray.

2. In a mixing bowl, whisk egg whites. In a separate bowl, combine flour, coconut, salt, and pepper.

3. Bread each shrimp by dipping in the egg whites and then placing in the bowl of flour and coconut. Toss shrimp in the bowl to coat, then carefully place on the Lid-it®. Arrange all breaded shrimp in a single layer. Spray the tops of the shrimp with a light coating of nonstick cooking spray.

4. Bake 5 minutes, flip, and bake an additional 5 to 6 minutes, or until golden brown.

TARA'S TRADITIONS *Jenn's kids love crunchy coconut shrimp, so she developed this healthy version in my ovenware. The kids can't get enough!*

Brunch

PREP TIME: 26 mins

COOK TIME: 30 mins

SERVES: 4

temp·tations
PRESENTABLE OVENWARE
by Tara
LID-IT®

Stuffed Banana Peanut Butter Pancakes

This is a great healthy breakfast that can be made quickly and enjoyed pre- or postworkout. Protein, complex carbs, good fat, and fruit! I eat either half or a whole pancake. Add more or less peanut butter or banana, depending on taste. Keeps my energy level high all morning long! You may also like to add a little cinnamon.

2½ cups all-purpose flour

2 tablespoons baking powder

1 teaspoon baking soda

1 teaspoon kosher salt

12 tablespoons (¾ cup) smooth peanut butter

4 tablespoons maple syrup

2½ cups buttermilk, well shaken

2 large eggs

1 tablespoon unsalted butter

2 small, ripe bananas, thinly sliced

1. Preheat oven to 250 degrees. Place temp-tations® Lid-it® in oven to preheat.

2. In a large bowl, whisk together flour, baking powder, baking soda, and salt until combined.

3. In another large bowl, whisk together peanut butter and maple syrup until smooth. Slowly whisk in buttermilk, then whisk in eggs until smooth.

4. Add peanut butter mixture to flour mixture, stirring just to combine. Preheat large nonstick pan over medium-high heat. Grease pan with some of the butter, add ¼ cup batter to pan, then place two slices of banana on pancake; top with 1 teaspoon additional batter.

5. Cook on first side until edges are set, lowering heat if getting too dark, 3 minutes. Flip and cook until puffed, 3 minutes more. Transfer pancakes to preheated Lid-it® and repeat with remaining batter.

TARA'S TRADITIONS *A favorite of Jenn's kids, Macaylan and Brodie, I have to admit the pairing of all these flavors makes me feel like a kid again!*

My big sister couldn't be more the opposite of me. Tracy was drawn more toward tube socks and black high-tops while you could never pull me away from a good Scarlett O'Hara dress. I wanted to wear those dresses everywhere. To the store, to the playground, bike riding... the lady in the store always told me that it wasn't appropriate to wear them everywhere but I obviously didn't agree. That big smile you see is because my mom finally allowed me to wear that beautiful dress to school for my first-grade photo and I felt just like a princess!

PREP TIME: 9 mins

COOK TIME: 30 mins

SERVES: 4

PRESENTABLE OVENWARE
by Tara

9-OZ MINI CASSEROLES

BRUNCH

Old World Green Eggs and Ham

This is a classic dish that I love to serve in individual casseroles for brunch or really anytime. I'm actually very reliable for eating what our family calls the "backwards banquet," things like steak for breakfast and pancakes for dinner.

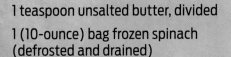

1 teaspoon unsalted butter, divided

1 (10-ounce) bag frozen spinach (defrosted and drained)

12 tablespoons (¾ cup) heavy cream

kosher salt

freshly ground pepper

½ cup black forest deli ham, cut into ½-inch pieces

4 large eggs

½ cup finely grated parmesan

pinch powdered nutmeg, for garnish

1. Preheat oven to 350 degrees. Butter 4 temptations® casseroles, set aside. Set a colander over a medium bowl.

2. In a large pan over medium-high heat melt ½ teaspoon butter and cook spinach until just wilted, 2 minutes.

3. Remove spinach to a colander, let cool and drain 3 minutes, pressing out any remaining liquid; chop coarsely.

4. Add 1 tablespoon heavy cream to each baker; season with salt and pepper. Divide the spinach and ham between the 4 bakers and crack an egg in each one. Top each egg with 2 tablespoons grated parmesan and remaining 2 tablespoons heavy cream.

5. Bake uncovered on middle rack until the whites are set and the cream is bubbling, 19 to 21 minutes. Garnish with nutmeg.

TARA'S TIDBITS™ *You can lighten this recipe by using low-fat cream and egg whites if you prefer. They also come out just as well in any other pattern, not just the Old World!*

Egg and Cheese Hamwich

Jenn, a dear friend of mine, is always so creative in the kitchen it's no wonder that she would spoil us with these great "hamwiches."

4 English muffins, split

4 slices American cheese

4 slices deli ham

4 large eggs

kosher salt

freshly ground black pepper

1 tablespoon unsalted butter

1. Preheat oven to 275 degrees. Place the English muffin bottoms into a 4-quart temp-tations® dish. Top each with a slice of cheese and a slice of ham. In the remaining two spaces in the dish, stack muffin tops to be heated.

2. Bake until warmed through and the cheese is melted, 10 minutes.

3. Meanwhile, beat the eggs in a medium bowl and season with ½ teaspoon salt and ¼ teaspoon pepper.

4. Melt butter in a medium nonstick skillet over medium heat. Add the eggs and use a wooden spoon to stir constantly until the eggs are cooked through and scrambled, about 5 minutes.

5. Divide the scrambled eggs among the muffin bottoms and top with the remaining muffin halves. Serve immediately.

TARA'S TIDBITS™ *To make Green Eggs and Cheese Hamwiches, add chopped fresh herbs, such as parsley and chives, to the eggs just before scrambling them.*

PREP TIME: 1 hour

COOK TIME: 40 mins

SERVES: 8

temp-tations.
PRESENTABLE OVENWARE
by Tara™

2.5 QUART

BRUNCH

Tara's Cream Cheese Cinnamon Rolls

You loved the Cinnamon Rolls in my last book and you asked to shorten the prep time by about 15 minutes. Mom and I listened and shortened the prep time by 60 minutes! We also decided to step into our family time machine, so now all the ingredients are old school and you should already have them in your cupboard.

6 tablespoons unsalted butter, melted, plus more for pan

8 ounces cream cheese, softened

1½ cups packed light brown sugar

2 teaspoons pure vanilla extract

2 tablespoons plus ½ teaspoon ground cinnamon

all-purpose flour for rolling

1 pound frozen white bread dough, thawed according to package directions

½ cup chopped pecans

2 teaspoons granulated sugar

1. Preheat oven to 350 degrees. Coat a 2.5-quart temp-tations® dish with butter and set aside.

2. In a large mixer bowl, beat the cream cheese on medium-high speed until light and fluffy, about 2 minutes. Add the brown sugar, 4 tablespoons butter, vanilla, and 2 tablespoons cinnamon and beat until smooth, about 2 minutes. Set aside.

3. On a lightly floured surface, roll the dough into a 16- x 10-inch rectangle. Spread the dough with the cream cheese mixture, leaving a ½-inch border, and sprinkle with pecans. Beginning with the longer side, gently roll the dough to form a log. Slice the log crosswise into eight 2-inch pieces and place in the prepared baking dish.

4. Cover with plastic wrap and let rise about 45 minutes, or until each roll doubles in thickness. Brush the tops of the rolls with remaining melted butter. Sprinkle with ½ teaspoon cinnamon and the granulated sugar.

5. Bake until the cinnamon rolls are cooked through and golden brown, 35 to 40 minutes. Let rest for 10 minutes before serving.

TARA'S TRADITIONS *This is my all-time favorite cinnamon roll recipe. It will turn out perfect every time, and it's so quick and easy to make. If you're thinking about selling your house, stick a batch in your oven!*

PREP TIME: 30 mins

COOK TIME: 30 mins

SERVES: 10

2.5 QUART

Not Just for Breakfast Bars

I LIVE on these bars when I'm exceptionally busy, especially when you seem to see me more than I see myself! I wanted a bar that didn't crumble and had a lot of flexibility—you can adapt this recipe to your liking—they store well, and keep fairly long unless you eat them all! I used to spend a small fortune on bars and I will never buy store-bought bars again.

1½ cups old-fashioned oats

¾ cup chopped walnuts

¾ cup almonds

3 tablespoons raisins

1 teaspoon ground cinnamon

¼ cup shredded coconut

⅓ cup chopped dried apricots

4 tablespoons unsalted butter

¼ cup honey

1 teaspoon vanilla extract

¾ cup brown sugar

1. Preheat oven to 350 degrees with a rack in the center. Place oats on a temp-tations® 2.5-quart dish and toast for 10 minutes. Add walnuts and almonds to the oats and toast for 10 more minutes.

2. In a large bowl, combine oat mixture with raisins, cinnamon, coconut, and apricots.

3. In a small skillet, melt butter, honey, vanilla extract, and brown sugar together. Pour butter mixture over the oat mixture, stirring to combine, until oat mixture is well coated.

4. Spread onto temp-tations® 2.5-quart dish. Using the back of a spoon, press the mixture firmly onto the bottom of the dish.

5. Let cool and cut into 10 bars (2 by 3.5 inches).

TARA'S TIDBITS™ *Quick, easy, delicious, and nutritious! Great for hikes, long road trips, camping, and lunch box snacks. Use whatever you have in your imagination or in your pantry. Some ingredients I've enjoyed adding were chocolate chips, coconut, pecans, almond slices, blueberries, dried cherries, dates, raisins, and M&M's.*

PREP TIME: 10 mins   **COOK TIME: 20 mins**   **SERVES: 6**   **EGG PLATTER**

temp-tations® Deviled Eggs

This dish has a spicy twist on the traditional classic. The Dijon and cayenne give it a nice slow burn that will delight your taste buds. Jenn brought these to a family potluck and they disappeared within minutes!

6 large eggs

5 tablespoons mayonnaise

1 teaspoon lemon juice

1 teaspoon Dijon mustard

pinch cayenne pepper

1 tablespoon fresh chives, thinly sliced

kosher salt

freshly ground pepper

1. Place eggs in a medium saucepot with enough cold water to cover by 1 inch. Bring eggs to a boil over high heat; boil 1 minute. Cover and remove from heat; let stand 10 minutes.

2. Drain eggs from water and run under cold water until completely cool to the touch.

3. Meanwhile, in a small bowl combine mayonnaise, lemon juice, mustard, cayenne pepper, and chives. Season with salt and pepper to taste; stir to combine.

4. Peel and slice eggs in half lengthwise, reserving whites and yolks. Place white halves cut side up on temp-tations® 10-inch egg platter. Gently crumble egg yolks into mayonnaise mixture. Stir to combine.

5. Dollop deviled egg mixture into egg white halves to fill by ½ inch.

TARA'S TRADITIONS *Jenn always thinks of the best finger foods, and although my family thinks these eggs are the best, it's difficult for us to convince Jenn to repeat any recipe twice. Jenn substitutes avocado for the mayonnaise or adds curry and a little sweet pickle.*

*Amy is my best friend, and her children Joey and Gracie are
my godchildren. Auntie Tara spoils them a bit, but her mother
and I also want to see that they eat well, so together we like to
invent recipes they love that are good for them. Amy and I look
forward to alone, "just us" girl time but I'm so happy for Amy.
She's renewing her vows with JT after 10 years of marriage!
That's amazing, but secretly I'm just happy to have an excuse
to head out to Colorado to spend time with them.*

PREP TIME: 7 mins

COOK TIME: 30 mins

SERVES: 10

temp·tations
PRESENTABLE OVENWARE
by tara
1 QUART

Amy's Vanilla Almond Granola

Amy and I came up with this recipe and it is absolutely wonderful. Several of my friends who typically don't care for granola love it. I eat it five or six times a week—as cereal, mixed with yogurt, or as a dry snack. Whenever I get a few minutes to myself I pull out my yoga mat and run to the studio with a big handful. I love granola!

Best comment I've gotten from one of my friends: "It's so expensive these days that I have tried and failed many recipes until now. The first time I made your granola, I made a huge batch. It was soooo good that I snacked on it nearly all day every day.

3 cups rolled oats (10 ounces)

1 cup chopped whole almonds (4 ounces)

4 tablespoons unsalted butter, cut into 4 pieces

½ cup orange blossom honey

½ teaspoon kosher salt

1 vanilla bean, split and scraped, or 1 tablespoon pure vanilla extract

1. Preheat oven to 300 degrees.

2. In a large bowl combine oats and almonds; set aside.

3. In a small saucepan over medium heat, melt butter, honey, and salt, stirring until dissolved, 3 minutes. Stir in vanilla.

4. Add butter–honey mixture to oat mixture, stirring well to combine. Transfer oats to a large non-stick baking sheet and spread into a single layer. Bake on middle rack until granola is golden brown, about 30 minutes, stirring every 10 minutes.

5. Cool granola on tray 12 minutes. Store in air-tight temp-tations® 1-quart dish up to one week.

TARA'S TRADITIONS *If you want to get the kids to eat it (I'm talking to you, Joey and Gracie), add 1 cup of chocolate chips or M&Ms or you can think about adding 1 cup of raisins and/or ½ cup of shredded coconut. It tastes like a healthy magic cookie bar.*

 PREP TIME: 10 mins

 COOK TIME: 15 mins

 SERVES: 6

 temp-tations
PRESENTABLE OVENWARE
by Tara
MUFFIN PAN

BRUNCH

Bimbi's Blueberry Buttermilk Corn Muffins

A morning visit to my second mother Bimbi isn't out of the ordinary, as I love to often share stories and our first cup of Saturday morning coffee together. If it's my lucky day, when I walk in her house it's filled with the most warm and delightful aroma that makes me want to sprint to her table.

¾ cup all-purpose flour, plus 2 tablespoons

½ cup stone ground cornmeal

¼ cup plus 1 tablespoon granulated sugar

2 teaspoons baking powder

½ teaspoon baking soda

½ teaspoon coarse salt

1 large egg

2 tablespoons honey

½ cup buttermilk, shaken

6 tablespoons melted unsalted butter

½ cup fresh blueberries (or frozen, rinsed, drained, and dried)

1. Preheat the oven to 400 degrees. Grease and flour a 6-cup temp-tations® muffin pan.

2. In a medium bowl, whisk flour, cornmeal, sugar, baking powder, baking soda, and salt. Make a well in the center of flour mixture.

3. Whisk egg and honey into buttermilk. Gently add buttermilk mixture to dry ingredients, then stir in butter until just combined. Do not overmix. Fold in blueberries.

4. Divide batter into muffin pan. Fill each muffin cup with heaping ⅓ cup batter. Bake until muffins are puffed and golden, 15 minutes, rotating halfway though.

5. Cool 10 minutes before unmolding.

TARA'S TIDBITS™ *Her famous made-from-scratch 10-minute muffins can be made ahead from ordinary ingredients that most everyone has in their pantry.*

 PREP TIME: 10 mins

 COOK TIME: 45 mins

SERVES: 10

 **temp-tations.** PRESENTABLE OVENWARE *by Tara* 1.7 QUART

Grandma Maria's Coffee Cake

Easy is always right! This is a quick cake based on modest ingredients that probably live in your pantry. You can substitute any seasonal fruit like apples, pears, or prunes.

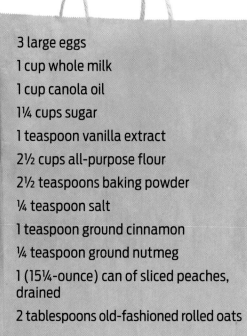

3 large eggs

1 cup whole milk

1 cup canola oil

1¼ cups sugar

1 teaspoon vanilla extract

2½ cups all-purpose flour

2½ teaspoons baking powder

¼ teaspoon salt

1 teaspoon ground cinnamon

¼ teaspoon ground nutmeg

1 (15¼-ounce) can of sliced peaches, drained

2 tablespoons old-fashioned rolled oats

1. Preheat oven to 350 degrees with rack in the center. Butter a temp-tations® 1.7-qt baker.

2. In a large bowl, whisk the eggs, milk, canola oil, sugar, and vanilla extract. In another bowl, whisk together the flour, baking powder, salt, cinnamon, and nutmeg.

3. Add the flour mixture to the egg mixture, stirring just until combined.

4. Pour the batter into the buttered pan. Arrange the peaches on top of the batter and top with oats.

5. Bake until golden brown, about 45 minutes.

TARA'S TRADITIONS *My grandmother Maria was known for her baked goods—really all her cooking—I think because she learned when she was just a little girl growing up in Austria. When she greeted us at her front door she was never without a hug, kiss and something to eat! The consummate hostess. This is one of her recipes I make often.*

PREP TIME: 10 mins

COOK TIME: 20 mins

SERVES: 4

4 QUART

Stuffed French Toast with Bananas and Nutella®

I really like this recipe because it's quick and super easy. SUPER easy!

unsalted butter for dish

2 ripe bananas

½ cup Nutella®

8 slices white or whole wheat bread, toasted

3 large eggs

¼ cup whole milk

1 tablespoon granulated sugar

confectioners' sugar for dusting

maple syrup

1. Preheat oven to 375 degrees. Lightly butter a 4-quart temp-tations® dish. Set aside.

2. Peel the bananas and slice them in half length wise. Slice each in half crosswise and slice each piece in half lengthwise, for a total of sixteen 4-inch slices.

3. Spread 1 tablespoon Nutella® hazelnut spread on each piece of bread. Top the bread with the banana slices and remaining bread.

4. In a separate large shallow bowl or baking dish, beat the eggs, milk, and 1 tablespoon of sugar together until lightly frothy. Coat each sandwich with the egg mixture on both sides, allowing the bread to absorb the egg mixture, then transfer to the buttered temp-tations® dish.

5. Bake until golden and cooked through, 20 minutes. Cool slightly before cutting each piece in half. Dust with confectioners' sugar and serve with maple syrup, if desired. Serve immediately.

TARA'S TRADITIONS *I'm watching my godchildren Brodie and Macaylan with their little plates turned upside down, and their auntie Tara is mortified that when Jenn rings my doorbell she'll find them in a food coma! They love Nutella® hazelnut spread, bananas, and French toast, so putting them all in one dish is a triple threat. You have got to try this one!*

BRUNCH

Spinach and Cheddar Fritatta

This dish is super easy to make, but looks likes you've been in the kitchen for hours. It is usually served for brunch and dinner also. I like to make this one ahead and serve it for Saturday family brunches with a colorful salad on the plate. It's always a big hit.

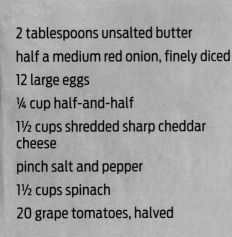

2 tablespoons unsalted butter

half a medium red onion, finely diced

12 large eggs

¼ cup half-and-half

1½ cups shredded sharp cheddar cheese

pinch salt and pepper

1½ cups spinach

20 grape tomatoes, halved

1. Preheat oven to 400 degrees.

2. Add butter to a large skillet and cook onions over medium-high heat until golden, 5 minutes.

3. In a large bowl, whisk eggs, half-and-half, cheese, salt, and pepper.

4. Add the vegetables to the eggs and pour the mixture into a greased temp-tations® pie dish.

5. Bake until egg is just set, 20 to 25 minutes.

TARA'S TIDBITS™ *Leftover frittata makes a great sandwich, either cold or warmed through. You can also substitute frozen egg whites for all those eggs and cut back on fat and calories.*

PREP TIME: 15 mins

COOK TIME: 20 mins

SERVES: 4

temp·tations
PRESENTABLE OVENWARE
by Tara

2 QUART

Hearty Breakfast Burrito

This is one of those hearty recipes that's great for those days when you (especially me ☺) just feel like treating ourselves to a bigger breakfast.

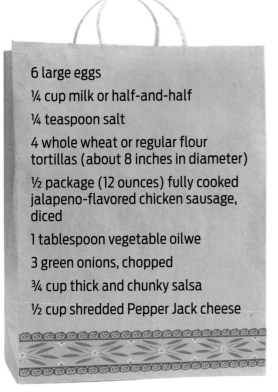

6 large eggs

¼ cup milk or half-and-half

¼ teaspoon salt

4 whole wheat or regular flour tortillas (about 8 inches in diameter)

½ package (12 ounces) fully cooked jalapeno-flavored chicken sausage, diced

1 tablespoon vegetable oilwe

3 green onions, chopped

¾ cup thick and chunky salsa

½ cup shredded Pepper Jack cheese

1. Preheat oven to 400 degrees. Spray a temp-tations® 2-quart dish with cooking spray.

2. In bowl, whisk together eggs, milk, and salt.

3. Stack flour tortillas, wrap in foil, and place in oven. In a 10-inch nonstick skillet over medium heat, cook sausage and green onions in hot oil, stirring occasionally, until lightly browned, 3 minutes. Add the eggs to the sausage mixture. Using a wooden spoon or heat-proof rubber spatula, stir the egg mixture, pushing it to the center and scraping the bottom and sides of skillet. Continue stirring until eggs thicken and set, about 2 minutes. Remove skillet from heat.

4. Remove tortillas from oven. Place one tortilla on work surface. Spoon one-fourth of egg mixture down center of tortilla, leaving a 1-inch border at either end. Fold ends up and over filling. Fold one side up and over filling and roll up. Place seam-side down in temp-tations® dish. Repeat with remaining egg mixture and tortillas.

5. Pour salsa over burritos and sprinkle with cheese. Bake until filling is warmed and cheese melts, 15 minutes.

TARA'S TIDBITS™ *A different way to start your day, have some fun, and experiment with whatever your family loves—like fried instead of scrambled eggs, bacon instead of (or in addition to) the chicken sausage, and refried beans topped with melted cheese. Ham or sausage may be substituted for the bacon. Serve with salsa on the side.*

PREP TIME: 12 mins   **COOK TIME: 30 mins**   **SERVES: 10**   **LID-IT®**

Bacon Cheddar Biscuits

This is a great unexpected-guest recipe to make ahead and freeze. I'll often grab one on my way to the studio, and by the time lunch rolls around it's thawed and makes a great meal next to a bowl of hearty soup or salad.

5 slices bacon

1 large egg yolk

¾ cup plus 1 tablespoon whole milk

2 cups all-purpose flour, plus more for dusting

1 tablespoon baking powder

2 tablespoons sugar

½ teaspoon kosher salt

¼ teaspoon freshly ground black pepper

6 tablespoons unsalted butter

4 ounces sharp yellow cheddar cheese (1¼ cups)

1. Preheat oven to 450 degrees.

2. Place bacon on a temp-tations® Lid-it® and cook until crisp, flipping bacon halfway through, 9 minutes. Remove to a paper towel to drain. Wipe grease from Lid-it®. Whisk together egg yolk and 1 tablespoon milk; set aside.

3. In a food processor with the blade attachment, combine flour, baking powder, sugar, salt, and pepper; pulse to combine. Add the butter and pulse until the size of large peas, then add the cheese and bacon; pulse 3 times. Add remaining milk, pulsing just to combine. Do not overmix.

4. Gently roll or press dough out between two sheets of parchment to 1-inch thickness. Using a floured 2½-inch biscuit cutter, cut 10 rounds of biscuits from dough, re-rolling dough once, if necessary. Chill biscuits in freezer on temp-tations Lid-it® 15 minutes.

5. Brush yolk mixture over biscuits and bake until golden, 20 to 25 minutes.

TARA'S TRADITIONS *This was one of our Sunday morning specialties. Mom always told me that it took more time to boil an egg than to make this recipe, and you'd be hard-pressed to find a better homemade biscuit anywhere. I find myself repeating that very same story to my niece and nephew Alexandra Maria and John David, when I bake Mom's favorite Bacon Cheddar Biscuits on Sunday mornings. We all agree, Mom's always right.*

BRUNCH

temp-tationista's Quichettes

Call your nearest temp-tationista BFFs to share these delightful savory brunch treats! Ask one of them to bring their muffin pan because this recipe requires two. Then relax, tune in, and catch David's Sunday show. We'll be watching out for you!

nonstick cooking spray

4 large eggs

1 cup half-and-half

1 sheet frozen puff pastry, thawed

½ cup shredded parmesan cheese

½ cup shredded mozzarella cheese

1 tomato, diced

¼ cup fresh spinach leaves, chopped (frozen okay if thawed and drained)

salt and pepper to taste

1. Preheat oven to 350 degrees. Spray muffin dish with nonstick cooking spray.

2. Unfold puff pastry and cut into 12 equal squares. Press 1 square into each cup of a muffin tin and prick the bottom a few times with a fork.

3. In a mixing bowl, beat the eggs and half-and-half until combined. Stir in parmesan cheese, mozzarella cheese, diced tomato, chopped spinach, and salt and pepper.

4. Divide the egg mixture evenly between the 12 pastry-lined muffin cups.

5. Bake 25 minutes, or until a toothpick inserted into the center of a quiche cup comes out mostly clean.

TARA'S TIDBITS™ *Serve warm or chilled. If you prefer another cheese instead of the combination of parmesan and mozzarella, you can substitute 1 cup of cheddar or Swiss. Add mushrooms, onions if you or the girls like them, and you may even enjoy adding. . . I'll fill in half the letters and let you guess the rest of this heavenly ingredient—d_v_n_ s_in_! Enjoy!*

Poultry

PREP TIME: 25 mins

COOK TIME: 45 mins

SERVES: 6

4 QUART

Chicken Enchiladas

Gone are the trips to the restaurant! Most Mexican dishes require a laundry list of ingredients, but this recipe keeps it simple without skimping on taste. Love that cleanup is so easy and it's a great family meal that everybody loves.

1 tablespoon olive oil, plus more for dish

½ cup sliced scallions

1 (4-ounce) can green chilies

1 cup sour cream

2 cups cubed or shredded cooked chicken breast

1 cup shredded cheddar cheese, divided

6 (12-inch) flour tortillas

¼ cup milk

1. Preheat oven to 350 degrees. Lightly oil a 4-quart temp-tations® dish. Set aside.

2. In a large pan over medium-high, heat oil. Add scallions and chilies; cook until soft. Reduce heat to low and stir in sour cream.

3. Remove ¾ cup of the sour cream mixture to a bowl and set aside. Add the chicken and ½ cup of the cheddar cheese to the pan and return to low heat, stirring to combine.

4. Fill each tortilla with chicken mixture. Tuck in sides of tortilla, roll up, and place in prepared dish, seam side down.

5. Whisk together the milk and the remaining ¾-cup portion of the sour cream mixture. Spoon over rolled tortillas and top with remaining cheddar cheese. Bake until hot and the cheese is bubbling, 30 to 35 minutes.

TARA'S TIDBITS™ *This is a great way to use leftover chicken! Serve with yellow rice and black beans or pinto beans. Garnish with sour cream and fresh, chopped tomatoes. I'm now embarrassed to have ever served my old enchilada recipe. ☺ This has become a weekly request.*

PREP TIME: 15 mins
COOK TIME: 20 mins
SERVES: 4

temp-tations
PRESENTABLE OVENWARE
by Tara
FOUR 9-OZ. CASSEROLES

POULTRY

Amy's Turkey Chili

This is a great, versatile recipe my best friend likes to prepare any time of the day or any day of the week. It can be served in sourdough bread bowls for a casual weekend get-together lunch or as an appetizer with a salad on the side.

½ tablespoon vegetable oil

½ small red onion, finely chopped (about ½ cup)

½ green pepper, chopped (about ½ cup)

8 ounces ground lean turkey

1 (14.5-ounce) can stewed tomatoes

1 (15.5-ounce) can red kidney beans, drained and rinsed

1 teaspoon crushed red chili pepper flakes

1 teaspoon ground cumin

½ teaspoon salt

1 cup shredded taco cheese blend (such as White Rose)

sour cream

tortilla chips

1. Preheat oven to 400 degrees.

2. In a large skillet, over medium-high, heat oil and cook red onion and green pepper until vegetables soften, 6 to 8 minutes. Add ground turkey and continue to cook until no longer pink, breaking up the turkey with a wooden spoon, 3 to 4 minutes.

3. Add the tomatoes, beans, chili flakes, cumin, and salt to combine. Divide chili mixture between 4 temp-tations® dishes. Bake in oven, covered, until heated through, 15 minutes.

4. Remove from oven and sprinkle each bowl of chili with cheese. Cover and let stand until cheese melts, 15 minutes. Serve warm with sour cream and tortilla corn chips, if desired.

TARA'S TIDBITS™ *You can also make this in a microwave: omit step one; and in step 2, cook in a microwave 5 minutes, until heated through. We use a Colby Monterey cheese blend with spices, but use your favorite shredded cheese or cheese blend. For a more unexpected kick, consider adding ½ teaspoon nutmeg and ¼ teaspoon ground cinnamon. Even if you use only two servings, make all four. They store well overnight in the refrigerator.*

Hunter's Chicken

This hearty dish is an old-time favorite that was traditionally cooked all day and served to hungry hunters home from the chase. Now temp-tations® makes this wonderful recipe quicker...with no hunting required!

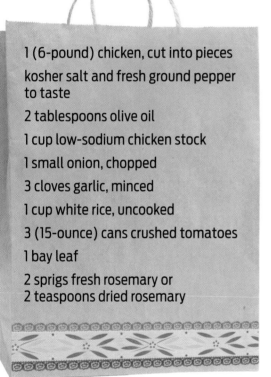

1 (6-pound) chicken, cut into pieces

kosher salt and fresh ground pepper to taste

2 tablespoons olive oil

1 cup low-sodium chicken stock

1 small onion, chopped

3 cloves garlic, minced

1 cup white rice, uncooked

3 (15-ounce) cans crushed tomatoes

1 bay leaf

2 sprigs fresh rosemary or
2 teaspoons dried rosemary

1. Preheat the oven to 350 degrees.

2. Wash the chicken and pat it dry. Season with salt and pepper.

3. In a large skillet over medium-high, heat 1 tablespoon of the oil until hot but not smoking. Cook the chicken until golden, about 5 minutes on each side. (Do not move the chicken once in the pan, except to turn it.)

4. Add the stock and cook until the liquid is reduced by half, 3 minutes. Transfer the chicken and juices to a temp-tations® 4-quart dish and set aside.

5. Wipe out the skillet, return to medium-high, and heat the remaining tablespoon of oil. Add the onions, garlic, and rice to the pan and stir to coat. Cook until the onions and garlic are softened and fragrant, about 2 minutes. Add the tomatoes, bay leaf, and rosemary and cook, stirring occasionally, 3 minutes more. Season to taste with the salt and pepper.

6. Pour the tomato mixture over the chicken, cover, and bake until the chicken pulls easily away from the bone, 40 minutes. Serve hot.

TARA'S TIDBITS™ *This is a great take-along casserole and also a great recipe to make for anyone who needs to feed a lot of hungry gentlemen.*

POULTRY

Jenn's Red Curry Chicken Chicken

If you've never had any Indian type of cuisine, this is a great one to start with because it's quick to prepare and so easy to follow. You probably won't have a few of these ingredients in your pantry, but I thought I'd share this more unusual recipe with you, where the hardest part is just finding these items at the store if it's your first time.

1 pound flat rice noodles

2 teaspoons sesame oil

1 tablespoon vegetable oil

1 tablespoon red curry paste

1 (14-ounce) can coconut milk

½ cup low-sodium chicken stock

2 tablespoons brown sugar

1 tablespoons fish sauce

1 pound boneless chicken, cut into bite-sized pieces

3 cups mixed vegetables, such as bell peppers, carrots, zucchini, onions, snap peas

12 small basil leaves, plus more for garnish, or ¼ teaspoon dried basil

1. Place the rice noodles in a wide, deep mixing bowl. Bring 6 quarts of water to a boil. Pour the boiling water over the rice noodles until they are completely submerged. As the noodles soften, gently stir them to loosen.

2. When the noodles are limp, taste to test for doneness, about 10 minutes. Drain and run under cold water to stop the cooking. Transfer to a temp-tations® 4-quart dish, toss with sesame oil, and set aside.

3. In a large skillet over medium-high, heat the vegetable oil. Add the curry paste and stir fry until fragrant, about 1½ minutes. Add the coconut milk and chicken stock, raise heat to medium-high, and bring to a simmer. Stir in the brown sugar and fish sauce.

4. Add the chicken and vegetables and simmer until the chicken is cooked through and the vegetables are tender. Just before serving, stir in the basil leaves.

5. Pour the chicken and vegetables over the rice noodles. Garnish with basil and serve.

TARA'S TIDBITS™ *If you can't find flat rice noodles, any shape will work— rice vermicelli, for instance. This is a great beginners curry, but always remember to make each recipe your own. You can substitute tofu for the chicken, for example, or switch up the vegetables—like your collection of temp-tations® presentable ovenware™, use your imagination, have fun, and create your very own traditions!*

PREP TIME: 10 mins **COOK TIME: 35 mins** **SERVES: 6** **4 QUART**

Herb Roasted Chicken Legs

As easy as this recipe is, you wouldn't think it would be so good! This is a great way to frugally feed a large gathering—and it's family friendly, too.

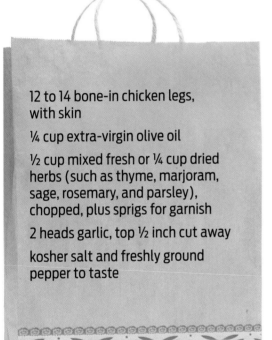

12 to 14 bone-in chicken legs, with skin

¼ cup extra-virgin olive oil

½ cup mixed fresh or ¼ cup dried herbs (such as thyme, marjoram, sage, rosemary, and parsley), chopped, plus sprigs for garnish

2 heads garlic, top ½ inch cut away

kosher salt and freshly ground pepper to taste

1. Preheat oven to 500 degrees.

2. Place the chicken legs in a 4-quart temp-tations® dish.

3. Pour the olive oil over the chicken and toss to coat the chicken.

4. Add the herbs and garlic and toss until distributed all over the chicken.

5. Roast until the skin is crisp and the juices run clear when the leg is pierced with a fork, about 35 minutes.

TARA'S TIDBITS™ *To achieve that nice lacquered look, baste the chicken legs every now and then with the juices that have collected in the pan.*
Add chili powder for a kick and serve along with your favorite bottled dipping sauce.

PREP TIME: 15 mins

 COOK TIME: 25 mins

 SERVES: 4

 temp·tations.
PRESENTABLE OVENWARE
by tara
4 QUART

Verona Chicken Parmesan

This is a delicious basic recipe, simple and quick, when you can't spend too much time figuring out what's for dinner. This is a great stand-by for your fussy guests. I can't think of any of my friends or family who don't love this one. It's also great the next day served on a roll for lunch.

POULTRY

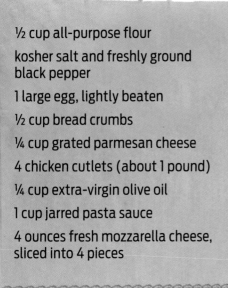

½ cup all-purpose flour

kosher salt and freshly ground black pepper

1 large egg, lightly beaten

½ cup bread crumbs

¼ cup grated parmesan cheese

4 chicken cutlets (about 1 pound)

¼ cup extra-virgin olive oil

1 cup jarred pasta sauce

4 ounces fresh mozzarella cheese, sliced into 4 pieces

1. Preheat oven to 350 degrees.

2. In a shallow bowl, season the flour with salt and pepper. Place egg in a separate shallow bowl. Place the bread crumbs and parmesan cheese in a third shallow bowl and stir to combine.

3. Dip each chicken cutlet into the flour mixture, then into the egg, letting the excess drip off, and then into the bread crumbs.

4. In a large skillet, over medium-high, heat olive oil. Add the chicken and cook, flipping once, until golden brown on both sides, about 6 minutes.

5. Transfer the chicken cutlets to a 4-quart temp-tations® dish. Pour the pasta sauce over the chicken and top with cheese. Bake until cooked through and the cheese is melted and bubbly, 15 to 20 minutes.

TARA'S TIDBITS™ *Whether it's in season or outside your back door in your garden, fresh basil makes a beautiful, tasty garnish. I love it on top of classic, plain old spaghetti, but any type of pasta or noodle is great served under the chicken with a simple salad on the side.*

Sticky Chipotle Wings

I made these for a Superbowl party last year and no one had any idea they were baked instead of fried; they polished off more than I thought was physically possible.

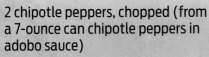

2 chipotle peppers, chopped (from a 7-ounce can chipotle peppers in adobo sauce)

1 tablespoon adobo sauce (from a 7-ounce can chipotle peppers in adobo sauce)

4 teaspoons honey

1 cup barbecue sauce

3 tablespoons soy sauce

2 teaspoons paprika

2 pounds party wings, or 2 pounds chicken wings, drumstick and wing tips separated

¼ cup chopped fresh cilantro, optional

1. In a small bowl combine the chopped chipotle peppers, adobo sauce, honey, barbecue sauce, soy sauce, and paprika. Pour ¾ cup of the marinade into a large resealable plastic bag. Add the chicken wings and toss to coat. Refrigerate the wings for 1 hour (or overnight, if desired). Reserve remaining marinade.

2. Preheat oven to 400 degrees. Arrange the wings in a single layer in a 4-quart temp-tations® dish. Discard the bag.

3. Roast wings for 40 minutes. Remove wings from the oven, flip over, and brush with the remaining marinade. Return the wings to the oven and continue roasting until they are slightly charred on top, 20 to 25 minutes.

4. Sprinkle with chopped cilantro, if desired, and serve immediately.

TARA'S TIDBITS™ *For an extra kick, try substituting smoked paprika for plain. Give this recipe to a friend so they can claim bragging rights, too!*

PREP TIME: 10 mins

COOK TIME: 50 mins

SERVES: 4

4 QUART

Grandma Maria's Sausage and Potato Casserole

The memory of walking into Grandma Maria's home on a snowy afternoon after a long day reminds me of this hearty casserole. It was the sweetest way I can think of to quickly defrost near-frostbitten fingers and toes.

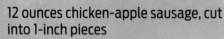

12 ounces chicken-apple sausage, cut into 1-inch pieces

12 ounces small red new potatoes, quartered

1 pound Brussels sprouts, trimmed and halved

2 tablespoons extra-virgin olive oil

kosher salt and freshly ground black pepper

4 sprigs fresh thyme, or 1½ teaspoons dried thyme leaves

1. Preheat oven to 400 degrees.

2. Place the sausage, potatoes, and Brussels sprouts in a 4-quart temp-tations® dish.

3. Add the olive oil, 1 teaspoon salt, ½ teaspoon pepper, and thyme; toss to coat.

4. Roast, tossing once halfway through cooking, until the potatoes are fork tender and browned in parts, 50 to 60 minutes. Serve immediately.

TARA'S TRADITIONS *You can throw this dish together rather quickly and it's perfect just as it is, but for more variety, if you prefer, different ingredient ideas can be green beans, onions, or even sliced apples. Grandma loved to serve her casserole alongside what she called "spaetzle," which means noodles in German.*

POULTRY

Baked Lemon Chicken

This is a flavorful, healthy, easily assembled dinner entrée. If you'd like to reserve time to share with your guests, the chicken can be put together with everything but the lemon juice and slices. Marinate for 3 hours in the fridge or overnight, adding the lemon juice and lemon slices when ready to cook.

5 tablespoons olive oil

4 garlic cloves, thinly sliced

2 teaspoons finely chopped fresh parsley

½ teaspoon sweet paprika

1 lemon, halved, one half very thinly sliced and the other half juiced

4 boneless skinless chicken breasts (2 pounds)

½ teaspoon kosher salt

¼ teaspoon fresh ground pepper

1 small red onion (6 ounces), halved and sliced into ¼-inch-thick slices

1. Preheat oven to 425 degrees.

2. In a 4-quart temp-tations® dish combine the olive oil, garlic, parsley, paprika, lemon slices, and 1 tablespoon lemon juice.

3. Season chicken with salt and pepper and add to dish, turning once to coat. Place onions and lemon slices around chicken, turning to coat.

4. Bake, basting occasionally, until the onions are soft and the chicken is cooked, 25 to 30 minutes.

5. Let rest 10 minutes before serving.

TARA'S TRADITIONS *I try to eat healthy, although it's against my nature.* ☺ *That's why I've used olive oil in this recipe instead of butter. When there are any leftovers, I always enjoy this chicken cold and cubed on top of a nice colorful salad for lunch.*

This is a photo of my mom in her twenties cooking for her favorite holiday—as you already know, Thanksgiving. You also know that she was my inspiration in creating temp-tations® presentable ovenware™. Life in and out of her kitchen would've been so much easier if I could just turn the clock back!
All of the steps Mom used to create her delicious Thanksgiving meals could've been prepped, cooked, served, and stored in just one dish!

PREP TIME: 15 mins

COOK TIME: 1 hour, 20 mins

SERVES: 4

temp·tations
PRESENTABLE OVENWARE
by Tara

4 QUART

POULTRY

Mom's Favorite Turkey Breast

I'm embarrassed to admit this, but this is the first time I ever cooked a turkey breast. No one makes a turkey as moist and so full of flavor as my mom does. Our entire family really enjoys this recipe—even the picky eaters claim this is the best turkey breast they ever had.

1 (3-pound) turkey breast

1 (2-pound) butternut squash, peeled, seeded, and cut into 1½-inch pieces

5 fresh sage leaves, or 2 tablespoons dried crumbled sage

3 tablespoons unsalted butter

1½ teaspoons kosher salt

½ teaspoon freshly ground black pepper

1. Preheat oven to 400 degrees. Place the turkey breast, skin side up, in a 4-quart temp-tations® dish. Place squash around the turkey.

2. Loosen the turkey skin and place the whole sage leaves or dried crumbled sage under the skin.

3. In a small saucepan, over medium heat, melt the butter and cook until just starting to brown, about 3 minutes. Immediately remove from heat. Brush the turkey all over with the browned butter and drizzle some of the browned butter over the squash. Season the turkey and squash with salt and pepper.

4. Roast, uncovered, tossing the squash once halfway through cooking, until an instant-read thermometer measures 165 degrees in the thickest part of the breast, 60 to 80 minutes.

5. Transfer the breast to a cutting board, cover loosely with foil, and let rest for 15 minutes. Slice thinly, transfer back to the dish, and serve with roasted squash.

TARA'S TRADITIONS *temp-tations® presentable ovenware™ lets you prepare the turkey and vegetables at the same time and in the same dish! I suspect the sage leaves might be Mom's secret to having this turkey breast turn out so moist and delicious.*

PREP TIME: 15 mins

COOK TIME: 20 mins

SERVES: 4

temp·tations.
PRESENTABLE OVENWARE
by Tara
4 QUART

JD's Fried Chicken Fingers

My nephew, John David, helped me make these. He loves chicken nuggets, so I thought we'd make them and bake them to look just like the ones you get from the drive-through, only healthier! These are the crispiest chicken fingers ever, and you can't tell the difference between these vs. fried.

POULTRY

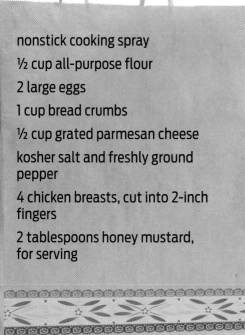

nonstick cooking spray

½ cup all-purpose flour

2 large eggs

1 cup bread crumbs

½ cup grated parmesan cheese

kosher salt and freshly ground pepper

4 chicken breasts, cut into 2-inch fingers

2 tablespoons honey mustard, for serving

1. Preheat oven to 425 degrees. Spray a temp-tations® 4-quart dish with nonstick cooking spray.

2. Pour flour onto a shallow plate. In another shallow dish, beat eggs.

3. Mix bread crumbs, cheese, salt, and pepper on a shallow plate.

4. Coat each piece of chicken with flour, then dip into egg mixture, letting excess drip off, then coat with breadcrumb mixture. Place on prepared dish.

5. Spray canola oil evenly over chicken and bake until chicken fingers are golden brown, 15 to 20 minutes. Serve with honey mustard on the side.

TARA'S TRADITIONS *All the kids request Auntie Tara to make these "chicken nuggets" when they come over; they've become a staple in my home now. We've invented all sorts of fun variations over the years. We put Popsicle sticks through them after they're cooked and put out a variety of dipping sauces like ketchup, honey mustard, and BBQ sauce. I love to use small letter cookie cutters—not only do we have fun with spelling the kids' names, but it's a great time for them to learn...and they don't even know it.*

PREP TIME: 30 mins

 COOK TIME: 40 mins

 SERVES: 8

 temp-tations.
PRESENTABLE OVENWARE
by tara
2 QUART

Laid-Back Chicken Potpie

This is the easiest potpie in the world to make. It definitely fits into the "comfort food" category, and leftovers are really delicious; they've always been a winter staple in our family.

2 tablespoons butter

1 tablespoon olive oil

1 onion, chopped

3 large carrots, chopped

3 large parsnips, chopped

1½ cups low-sodium chicken stock

2 tablespoons all-purpose flour

½ cup reduced-fat cream

zest of 1 lemon

kosher salt and freshly ground pepper to taste

1 (5-pound) roasted chicken, meat removed to make about 3 cups

1 tablespoon chopped fresh tarragon

1 sheet frozen puff pastry, thawed and rolled out to a 9½ by 11-inch rectangle

all-purpose flour for dusting

1 lightly whisked egg white

1. Preheat the oven to 350 degrees. In a large skillet, over medium-high, heat the butter and oil. Add the onions and cook until fragrant and soft, about 3 minutes. Add the carrots and parsnips and cook, stirring occasionally, until softened, about 10 minutes.

2. Turn the heat up to high, add ½ cup of the stock, and simmer until reduced by half, 5 to 7 minutes. Reduce the heat to low, add the flour, and cook, stirring constantly, for 2 minutes. Add the cream and 1 cup of the chicken stock and cook, stirring, until heated through. Add the lemon zest and stir. Season generously with salt and pepper. Add the chicken and tarragon and stir to thoroughly combine.

3. Preheat the oven to 375 degrees. Generously flour a clean work surface and a rolling pin. Roll out the puff pastry sheet into as close to a square as possible, about ⅛-inch thick. Transfer the chicken mixture to a temp-tations® 2-quart dish. Drape the puff pastry over it, allowing it to overhang the edges. Trim the dough to within ½ inch of the edge of the dish. Pinch the dough together at 1-inch intervals to create a crust. Brush all over with the egg white.

4. Bake until the crust is golden and flaky and chicken is hot, about 30 minutes.

TARA'S TIDBITS™ *This is also a great recipe for freezing—take it out of the freezer in the morning, let it defrost in the oven, set your time, and bake. You'll have a ready, homemade meal when you walk in the door from work! Enjoy—it's a great dish!*

PREP TIME: 15 mins

COOK TIME: 35 mins

SERVES: 4

temp·tations.
PRESENTABLE OVENWARE
by tara
2 QUART

Cozy Chicken Casserole

This recipe makes wonderful use of kitchen staples and is very easy to prepare. This family favorite is a meal by itself, but great served with crusty bread or a tossed salad.

8 ounces fusilli pasta

2 tablespoons butter

1 pound boneless, skinless chicken breasts, chopped

3 tablespoons all-purpose flour

2 cups milk

1 chicken bouillon cube

¼ teaspoon white pepper

1 (10-ounce) bag frozen baby broccoli florets

½ cup shredded carrots

1¼ cups shredded sharp cheddar cheese

1. Bring a large pot of salted water to a boil. Boil the pasta for 2 minutes less than the package directions. Drain and transfer to a 2-quart temp-tations® dish.

2. Meanwhile, preheat oven to 375 degrees. In a large skillet over medium-high heat, melt the butter. Add the chopped chicken and sauté until browned, about 5 minutes.

3. Whisk the flour into the milk and add to the skillet along with the chicken bouillon cube and white pepper. Stir until the bouillon cube is melted and sauce is bubbling and thick.

4. Stir in broccoli florets, shredded carrots, and half of the cheddar cheese. Pour over the pasta in the dish and lightly stir to combine.

5. Top casserole with the remaining half of the cheddar cheese, and bake just until casserole is bubbly hot and cheese is beginning to brown, 20 minutes. Let cool 5 minutes before serving.

TARA'S TIDBITS™ *Try using bowtie pasta for an added variation and add different vegetables...like spinach.*

Berry Good Spinach Salad

A refreshingly different salad. Use any berry you have on hand.

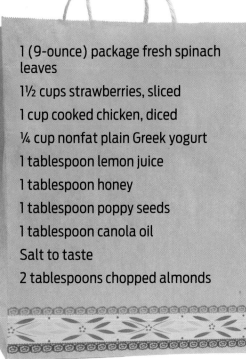

1 (9-ounce) package fresh spinach leaves

1½ cups strawberries, sliced

1 cup cooked chicken, diced

¼ cup nonfat plain Greek yogurt

1 tablespoon lemon juice

1 tablespoon honey

1 tablespoon poppy seeds

1 tablespoon canola oil

Salt to taste

2 tablespoons chopped almonds

1. In a large temp-tations® bowl, combine spinach leaves, strawberries, and diced chicken.

2. In a separate bowl whisk together the yogurt, lemon juice, honey, poppy seeds. In a slow stream whisk in the canola oil until the dressing is smooth. Season with salt to taste.

3. Drizzle dressing over the salad in the bowl and toss gently until well mixed.

4. Top with chopped almonds and serve.

TARA'S TIDBITS™ *Use any bottle of store-bought dressing of your choice if you're pressed for time. So easy!*

PREP TIME: 18 mins

COOK TIME: 18 mins

SERVES: 4

temp·tations.
PRESENTABLE OVENWARE
by Tara
1.5 QUART

Whimsy Chicken Fried Rice

This recipe has just about every kid's stamp of approval, and the best part is they don't even know it's good for them! It's quick, it's easy, and it's a lot of fun to make. I call it whimsy because you can always keep this recipe interesting with so many different additions, including leftovers.

POULTRY

2 tablespoons plus 1 teaspoon soy sauce

1 tablespoon plus 1 teaspoon sesame oil

2 to 3 teaspoons Asian chili sauce or hot sauce

2 large eggs, lightly beaten

kosher salt

3 tablespoons vegetable oil

1 (8-ounce) chicken breast, cut into 1-inch pieces

2 cloves garlic, finely chopped

5 scallions, white and light green parts, thinly sliced, divided

4 cups cooked long-grain rice (such as Jasmine rice)

½ cup frozen peas, defrosted

1. In a small bowl combine the soy sauce, 1 tablespoon sesame oil, and chili sauce; set aside. Whisk remaining 1 teaspoon sesame oil with eggs and season with a pinch of salt.

2. In a wok or large nonstick skillet, over medium-high, heat 1 teaspoon vegetable oil. Add eggs and cook, stirring often, until scrambled, about 30 seconds. Remove eggs to a temp-tations® 1.5-quart dish and set aside; reserve pan.

3. Return pan to medium high and add remaining vegetable oil. When almost smoking, add chicken and cook, stirring often, 3 minutes. Add garlic and white parts of scallions; cook, stirring, 2 minutes. Add rice, stirring to coat, and cook 1½ minutes.

4. Add sauce and peas, stirring often until rice is coated and chicken is just cooked, 1 minute. Add scrambled egg and scallion tops, tossing to combine.

5. Transfer back to a temp-tations® 1.5-quart bowl and serve warm.

TARA'S TIDBITS™ *I can go on forever with countless substitutions and additions. Just a few suggestions that I like are scrambled eggs with bacon; any vegetable like corn, water chestnuts, carrots, and onions; sometimes I'll even add shrimp and ham. If you have a rotisserie chicken, that's always a great time-saver and so is picking one up at the store.*

Honey Sesame Chicken

Great cupboard ingredient recipe—awesome and easy!

4 large boneless, skinless, chicken breasts (8 ounces each)

1 tablespoon jarred minced garlic

2 tablespoons honey

2 teaspoons soy sauce

2 teaspoons sesame oil

Toasted sesame seeds, for garnish, optional

1. Add chicken breasts, garlic, honey, soy sauce, and sesame oil to a food storage bag, and toss to combine. Refrigerate for 1 hour to marinate.

2. Preheat oven to 375 degrees.

3. Remove chicken from marinade and place on a 4-quart temp-tations® dish. Bake, flipping halfway through, until chicken is cooked, 25 to 30 minutes.

4. Garnish with toasted sesame seeds.

TARA'S TIDBITS™ *Add a touch of cayenne pepper for an eye opener and pineapple if you want to feel like you're on stay-cation!*

PREP TIME: 30 mins

COOK TIME: 1+ hour

SERVES: 4

PRESENTABLE OVENWARE
by Tara™
4 QUART

Lisa's Squash & Turkey Lasagna

Pure garden goodness! Healthy alternative to the traditional lasagna – the kids love it and it's as good reheated the next day!

nonstick cooking spray

1 pound ground turkey

½ diced yellow onion

¾ teaspoon Italian seasoning

¼ teaspoon salt

¼ teaspoon pepper

2 cups prepared spaghetti sauce

2 to 3 large zucchini

3½ cups peeled and cubed butternut squash

15 ounces part-skim ricotta cheese

2 large egg whites

½ teaspoon dried oregano

2 tablespoons parmesan cheese

2 teaspoons minced garlic

1½ cups mozzarella cheese

1. Preheat oven to 325 degrees. Spray a temptations® 4-quart dish with nonstick cooking spray. Spray a large nonstick skillet with nonstick cooking spray and place over medium-high heat. Add the ground turkey, yellow onion, Italian seasoning, salt, and ⅛ teaspoon of pepper, and sauté until meat is browned, about 8 minutes.

2. Spread half of the meat mixture over the bottom of the greased dish and top with half of the spaghetti sauce.

3. Thinly slice the zucchini lengthwise (a mandolin works best for this, but be careful!) and then place a full layer of slices, slightly overlapping, over the sauce in the dish. Layer one third of the butternut squash into the dish.

4. In a mixing bowl, combine ricotta cheese, egg whites, oregano, parmesan cheese, garlic, and ⅛ teaspoon of pepper. Using half of the ricotta mixture, drop dollops over the zucchini layer and top with one third of the butternut squash. Top with half of the mozzarella cheese.

5. Repeat all to make another layer by first spreading remaining meat mixture, followed by; tomato sauce, zucchini, ricotta mixture, butternut squash and then finally mozzarella cheese.

6. Cover with foil and bake 45 minutes. Raise oven temperature to 350 degrees. Uncover and bake an additional 25 to 30 minutes. Let cool 10 minutes before slicing.

TARA'S TIDBITS™ *Throw noodles in if you like—or anything else. Make it your family favorite!*

Traditional Cobb Salad

When it's way too hot to cook, this salad is perfect! I love ordering Cobb salads out, but this fresh salad at home is even more fabulous.

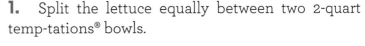

6 ounces chopped lettuce mix

2 (6-ounce) chicken breasts, cooked and chopped

¼ cup crumbled Gorgonzola cheese

6 slices turkey bacon, cooked and chopped

1 cup chopped broccoli

4 green onions, chopped

1 large tomato, chopped

1 avocado, chopped

COBB DRESSING

¼ cup mayonnaise

2 tablespoons red wine vinegar

1 tablespoon water

2 teaspoons Dijon mustard

½ teaspoon Worcestershire sauce

¼ teaspoon garlic powder

⅛ teaspoon celery salt

⅛ teaspoon pepper

1. Split the lettuce equally between two 2-quart temp-tations® bowls.

2. Top the lettuce in each bowl with an equal amount of chicken, Gorgonzola, bacon, broccoli, green onions, tomato, and avocado.

3. Make the dressing: In a separate large bowl, whisk the mayonnaise, red wine vinegar, water, mustard, Worcestire, garlic powder, celery salt, and pepper together until combined.

4. Divide dressing between salads and toss to coat. Serve immediately.

TARA'S TIDBITS™ *Use roasted chicken for an even quicker preparation time.*

Meats

PREP TIME: 15 mins

COOK TIME: 1 hour

SERVES: 8

temp·tations.
PRESENTABLE OVENWARE
by tara
2 QUART

Wrigley Hot Dog Casserole

Great for kids and the young at heart! There are so many regional variations of the all-American hot dog, but I chose to use this one for this recipe because it makes a striking casserole. Its inspiration came from "The Chicago Dog," a Wrigley Field staple.

MEATS

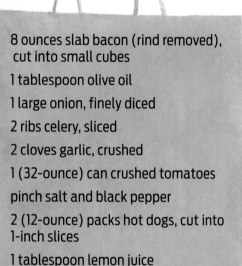

8 ounces slab bacon (rind removed), cut into small cubes

1 tablespoon olive oil

1 large onion, finely diced

2 ribs celery, sliced

2 cloves garlic, crushed

1 (32-ounce) can crushed tomatoes

pinch salt and black pepper

2 (12-ounce) packs hot dogs, cut into 1-inch slices

1 tablespoon lemon juice

½ cup fresh basil, shredded (optional)

1. Preheat oven to 400 degrees.

2. In a medium skillet, over medium-high heat, cook the bacon until the fat renders, 5 minutes, then remove the bacon and discard half the fat.

3. Cook the onions and celery in the remaining fat over medium heat for 5 minutes. Add the garlic and cook one more minute.

4. Add the tomatoes, bacon, stock, salt, pepper, and hot dogs and bring to boil.

5. Transfer to casserole and bake, stirring halfway through, for 40 minutes. Stir in lemon juice and basil before serving.

TARA'S TIDBITS™ *Make sure you serve this with plenty of crusty bread, or even mashed potatoes—as long as you have something to mop up the juices. If you'd like, you could also sprinkle grated parmesan cheese on top, just for fun.*

Imperial Meatballs

Can be premade and served over rice, or wrapped in lettuce with pineapple chunks and green bell peppers as a refreshing roll. For extra zing, try dipping the meatballs in a sweet Asian chili sauce (Thai sauce is a great example) that you'll easily find in your local grocery store. Also consider garnishing with fresh cilantro.

canola oil for dish

1½ pounds lean ground pork

½ cup panko bread crumbs

3 scallions, thinly sliced

1 large egg

3 tablespoons soy sauce

1 tablespoon grated fresh ginger (recommended) or 1½ teaspoons powdered ginger

2 cloves garlic, minced

1 tablespoon toasted sesame oil

2 teaspoons sugar

1. Preheat oven to 400 degrees. Lightly brush a 4-quart temp-tations dish with canola oil and set aside.

2. In a large bowl, place the pork, bread crumbs, and half of the scallions. Do not mix.

3. In a small bowl, mix the egg, soy sauce, ginger, garlic, sesame oil, and sugar until combined. Pour the wet mixture over the pork. Using your hands, gently combine the meat with the wet ingredients, being careful not to overwork the meat.

4. Form 1½-inch round meatballs and place in the prepared dish.

5. Bake until cooked through and browned, 25 to 30 minutes. Sprinkle with the remaining scallions.

TARA'S TRADITIONS *This is one of those lazy stay-at-home Sunday recipes that always makes me smile and reminds me of my irreplaceable two dads. I can still hear them saying (practically in stereo) every time I left the TV room for my required second batch of meatballs, "We've got to stop 'sampling' these before the game even starts!" When I walked back into the room to replace the first empty tray of crumbs, I just loved watching their guilty faces, and thought about making a third.*

Maple Glazed Baby Back Ribs

Raise your hand if you'd like to be the most popular girl at the party! I served these at a tailgating party and got loads of lip-smacking rave reviews. I was told they were a refreshing change from the traditional BBQ baby back ribs.

¼ cup light brown sugar

2 tablespoons kosher salt

2 tablespoons smoked sweet paprika, divided

1 tablespoon garlic powder

3 teaspoons mustard powder

3 pounds baby back ribs

½ cup maple syrup

½ cup apple cider vinegar

1 tablespoon Worcestershire sauce

3 tablespoons ketchup

1. In a small bowl, combine the brown sugar, salt, 1 tablespoon of the paprika, the garlic powder, and mustard; whisk to combine. Reserve 1 tablespoon of the spice mix. Coat the ribs on both sides with the remaining spice rub. Marinate the ribs in the dry rub for 1 hour. Wrap the ribs tightly in foil and place them, meaty-side-down, in a 4-quart temp-tations® dish.

2. Preheat oven to 325 degrees with oven rack in the upper third of the oven. Bake until the meat is tender, about 2 hours.

3. While the ribs bake, in a small saucepan, combine the maple syrup, cider vinegar, and Worcestershire sauce over low heat until warm. Cover and keep warm.

4. Remove the ribs from the oven and raise the heat to 450 degrees. Remove the foil (and reserve) from the ribs and pour off any accumulated juices. Return the ribs to the foil and brush with the maple syrup mixture ending with the meaty side up. Reserve the remaining maple syrup mixture. Place the ribs meaty-side-up on the foil and dust with the reserved dry rub. Roast until the ribs are lacquered and the edges are crisp, 10 to 15 minutes.

5. Combine the remaining 1 tablespoon of smoked paprika, the ketchup, and the remaining maple syrup mixture in a small saucepan and bring to a simmer. Serve alongside the ribs.

TARA'S TIDBITS™ *For a time-saver, you can always marinate the day before you plan on serving the ribs. I sometimes make extra glaze and place it in a ketchup bottle for basting the ribs. Soooo yummy.*

Tara's Pork Chops with Apples and Onions

WILL NEVER SHAKE & BAKE AGAIN! This recipe has the look and taste of a special-occasion meal, but without all the work. I love the perfect combination of the sweet and savory of the apples and onions.

MEATS

4 bone-in pork chops, cut ¾-inch thick

kosher salt and freshly ground black pepper

1 tablespoon butter

2 tablespoons extra-virgin olive oil

2 tablespoons grainy Dijon mustard

1 tablespoon fennel seeds

2 medium onions, sliced into half moons

3 baking apples, such as Honeycrisp, Jonagold, Granny Smith, or Braeburn, cored and each sliced into 8 wedges

1 cup apple cider

1 teaspoon fresh thyme, plus sprigs for garnish, or ½ teaspoon dried

1. Preheat oven to 375 degrees. Season pork with salt and pepper. In a large nonstick skillet over medium-high, heat the butter and one tablespoon of the olive oil. Add the pork and cook until both sides are brown, turning once, about 5 minutes. Reserve pan. Transfer the pork to a plate to cool slightly. Spread the mustard on one side of each pork chop and press the fennel seeds into each.

2. Add the remaining 1 tablespoon of olive oil to the skillet over medium heat; add the onions, apples, and thyme. Cook until the apples are golden and slightly softened, 5 to 7 minutes.

3. Place the pork chops and their juices in a 4-quart temp-tations® dish and season with salt and pepper. Spread the apple mixture evenly over them. Add the apple cider and bake until the pork is tender, and a meat thermometer inserted into the center registers 150 degrees, about 15 minutes. Garnish with the thyme sprigs. Serve warm over rice with a spoonful of the apple mixture on top.

TARA'S TIDBITS™ *Using a wide variety of apples is like throwing your taste buds their own private party. Honeycrisp apples are among the best cooking apples, as they don't fall apart at high temperatures. Jonagolds, Granny Smiths, and Braeburns also make excellent baking apples.*

Roasted Sausage and Grapes

LOVE AT FIRST BITE! This is a shockingly delicious, easy weeknight dish but impressive enough for company. I love it because it's prepared and baked in the same ovenware, so cleanup is a cinch.

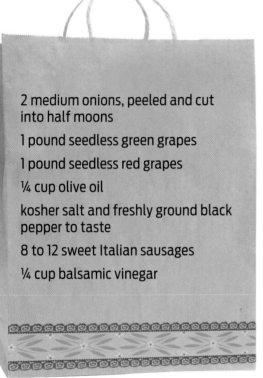

2 medium onions, peeled and cut into half moons

1 pound seedless green grapes

1 pound seedless red grapes

¼ cup olive oil

kosher salt and freshly ground black pepper to taste

8 to 12 sweet Italian sausages

¼ cup balsamic vinegar

1. Preheat oven to 375 degrees. Combine the onions and grapes in a 4-quart temp-tations® dish. Add the olive oil and toss to thoroughly coat. Season with salt and pepper.

2. Tuck the sausages into the dish, nestling them among the grape and onion mixture. Roast until the sausages are browned and crisp, or until the juices run clear when a sausage is poked with a fork, 45 minutes to 1 hour. Sprinkle the sausages with the balsamic vinegar and serve warm.

MEATS

TARA'S TIDBITS™ *A sprinkle of balsamic vinegar brightens this sweet and savory meal and is sure to have your mouth watering. If you'd like to add some contrast to this meal, use spicy Italian sausage instead of sweet. Serve with bread, fresh foccacia, or ciabiatta if you can find it. It will make you feel as though you're sitting in a tiny Mediterranean café. Buon Appetito!*

Tara's Individual Meat Loaves

This is a "Where have you been all my life?" recipe. A friend has a very picky eater for a son. When she involved him in preparing their meals, he not only cleaned his plate but also constantly wanted to repeat his performance for his friends! These adorable individual meat loaves can be prepared ahead of time and frozen...just minutes to the table. Who doesn't love meat loaf?

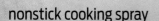

nonstick cooking spray

1 tablespoon vegetable oil

3 slices bacon, stacked and cut into thirds

1 small onion, finely chopped

¼ pound mushrooms, trimmed and finely chopped

1¼ pound lean ground beef

1 cup fresh whole wheat bread crumbs, from 2 slices of bread

¾ teaspoon salt

½ teaspoon plus ⅛ teaspoon ground pepper

1 large egg

1 (14.5 ounce) can diced tomatoes with garlic and olive oil, divided

2 tablespoons plus 2 teaspoons drained horseradish, divided

1. Preheat oven to 350 degrees. Spray a temp-tations® dish with nonstick cooking spray.

2. In 10-inch skillet over medium high, heat oil. Cook bacon pieces until browned and crisp, turning once, 5 to 8 minutes. With tongs, remove bacon to paper towel to drain, reserve pan. Return skillet to medium-high, add onion and cook 5 minutes then add mushrooms and cook, stirring occasionally, until vegetables are tender, 5 minutes. Remove pan from heat and set aside to cool onion mixture.

3. In bowl combine beef, bread crumbs, salt, ½ teaspoon pepper, and onion mixture. In a small bowl, whisk egg, ½ cup diced tomatoes with juice and 2 tablespoons horseradish; stir into beef mixture. Evenly divide beef mixture and press into the 6 muffin cups.

4. Bake until meat thermometer inserted in center of meatloaves registers 160 degrees, 40 minutes. Meanwhile, in small saucepan over high heat, combine remaining diced tomatoes, 2 teaspoons horseradish and ⅛ teaspoon of pepper. Bring to a boil, then reduce heat to low; cover and simmer 2 minutes.

5. Turn out meatloaves and place one on each plate. Spoon some tomato sauce on top of each meatloaf. Garnish each with 2 pieces of bacon.

TARA'S TRADITIONS *My friend who passed along this recipe loved to cook for children and sometimes used ketchup to write their initials on top of their very own meatloaf and stood little broccoli "trees" and "copper pennies" (carrot slices browned on the stovetop with honey and butter) next to them.*

 PREP TIME: 30 mins

 COOK TIME: 3 hours

 SERVES: 4

 temp-tations.
PRESENTABLE OVENWARE
by Tara

3 QUART

Tara's Traditional Pot Roast

You can substitute a cup of broth or even water for the red wine and still provide the needed moisture to tenderize the meat. Either way, this inexpensive cut will be so tender you can pull it apart with your fork! If you're feeling adventurous, you might even choose to replace the cup of red wine with a cup of grape juice and a tablespoon of red wine vinegar, or a can of cola-flavored carbonated beverage. I love it served with mashed potatoes and asparagus.

MEATS

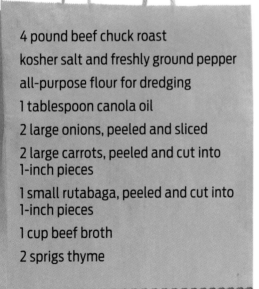

4 pound beef chuck roast

kosher salt and freshly ground pepper

all-purpose flour for dredging

1 tablespoon canola oil

2 large onions, peeled and sliced

2 large carrots, peeled and cut into 1-inch pieces

1 small rutabaga, peeled and cut into 1-inch pieces

1 cup beef broth

2 sprigs thyme

1. Preheat oven to 350 degrees. Season the meat on both sides with salt and pepper and then dredge in flour.

2. In a large skillet, over medium-high, heat the oil and brown the meat well on all sides.

3. Transfer the beef to a 3-quart temp-tations® dish, reserve pan. Add the onions, carrots, and rutabaga to the pan and cook for about 5 minutes.

4. Transfer vegetables to dish with beef, surrounding the pot roast. Add the thyme and beef broth. Season with salt and pepper.

5. Cover and cook until meat is tender, about 3 hours.

TARA'S TRADITIONS *There is just something so warm and homey about pot roast. You can dress it up or dress it down—either way it's delicious. This recipe has been handed down in my family for generations. There's nothing fancy about it, it's just plain good. This is the meal everyone asked for when we were nor'easter housebound. Not only because it's so darn good but also because we knew all of the ingredients were already in our pantries.*

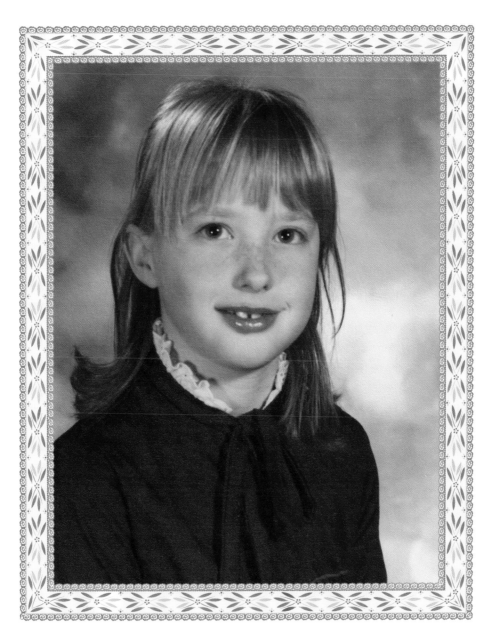

This photo was taken when I was about eight years old, and what I remember most from that time what how my friends were always invited to dinner. Dinner was always important to my family. Family has always been important, and we're really good about sharing our feelings. Sitting around the table for us is a time to reconnect. Mom's rule at our table was we had to try everything. We didn't have to like it but we had to try it. We—friends included—were also never allowed to say "yuck!" We had a big dining room table and there was rarely an empty seat in the house. Memories like this led me to create temptations®. It's all about sharing and laughing: sharing and laughing over something that, no matter what mood you're in, makes you happy.... FOOD!

Orange Glazed Pork Roast

There is just something so warm and homey about pork roast. You can dress it up or dress it down—either way it's delicious.

nonstick cooking spray

3 pounds boneless pork loin roast

½ teaspoon salt

¼ teaspoon pepper

½ teaspoon zest plus 1 tablespoon juice, from 1 orange

2 green onions, chopped

⅓ cup orange marmalade

1 tablespoon minced fresh gingerroot

1 teaspoon reduced sodium soy sauce

MEATS

1. Preheat oven to 450 degrees. Spray temp-tations® 4-quart dish with cooking spray. Sprinkle pork roast with salt and pepper. Place in dish and roast 15 minutes. Reduce oven temperature to 325 degrees.

2. Meanwhile, in a small bowl, combine orange zest, juice, green onions, marmalade, ginger, and soy sauce; stir to combine.

3. Brush pork with marmalade mixture and return pork to oven. Cook the pork, basting several times with marmalade mixture, until a meat thermometer inserted in thickest part of the roast registers 160 degrees, about 35 to 40 minutes. Cover with foil and let stand 10 minutes before carving.

TARA'S TIDBITS™ *If you're a fan of rosemary, you can give this recipe an extra kick by mixing about a tablespoon of fresh or dried rosemary into the orange glaze and even using fresh rosemary sprigs for garnish. As I always say, we eat with our eyes first, so don't be afraid to get those bonus points for presentation with a little garnish!*

PREP TIME: 10 mins

COOK TIME: 15 mins

SERVES: 4

temp-tations.
PRESENTABLE OVENWARE
by Tara
LID-IT©

Mom's Ham Steaks with Glazed Pineapple

Sweet vs. salty = DIVINE!!!

MEATS

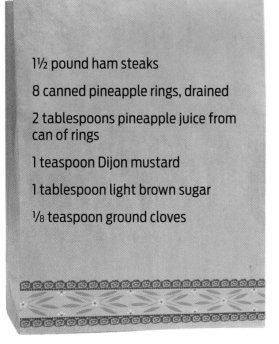

1½ pound ham steaks

8 canned pineapple rings, drained

2 tablespoons pineapple juice from can of rings

1 teaspoon Dijon mustard

1 tablespoon light brown sugar

⅛ teaspoon ground cloves

1. Preheat oven to 375 degrees. Line a Lid-it® with aluminum foil.

2. Place ham steaks on the lined Lid-it® and arrange pineapple rings on top.

3. In a small bowl, whisk together pineapple juice, Dijon mustard, brown sugar, and ground cloves. Drizzle over the pineapple-topped ham steaks.

4. Bake just until ham steaks are warmed throughout and glaze is beginning to brown, 10 to 15 minutes. Serve immediately.

TARA'S TIDBITS™ *Don't have any pineapple juice on hand? Use orange juice, pomegranate, or any preserves with a little water!*

PREP TIME: 20 mins

COOK TIME: 40 mins

SERVES: 4

2 QUART

Tara's Stuffed Peppers

LOVE LOVE LOVE! You can use all one color peppers or one of each (red, green, yellow, and orange) for a colorful table.

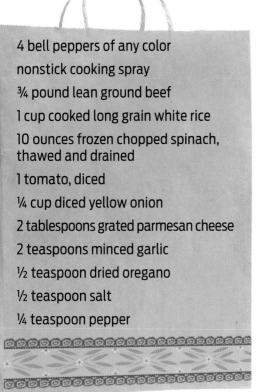

4 bell peppers of any color

nonstick cooking spray

¾ pound lean ground beef

1 cup cooked long grain white rice

10 ounces frozen chopped spinach, thawed and drained

1 tomato, diced

¼ cup diced yellow onion

2 tablespoons grated parmesan cheese

2 teaspoons minced garlic

½ teaspoon dried oregano

½ teaspoon salt

¼ teaspoon pepper

1. Preheat oven to 350 degrees. Remove tops from bell peppers, scoop out and discard seeds. Spray the outside of peppers with nonstick cooking spray.

2. In a mixing bowl, combine beef, rice, spinach, tomato, onion, parmesan, garlic, oregano, salt, and pepper. Mix well to combine.

3. Fill each pepper with an equal amount of the filling and then place into a 2-quart temp-tations® dish.

4. Bake just until a meat thermometer inserted into the filling registers 160 degrees, 35 to 45 minutes. Serve immediately.

MEATS

TARA'S TIDBITS™ *Leave out the beef for a vegetarian version!*

Heavenly Ham and Potato Casserole

Total comfort food – great way to use leftover ham!

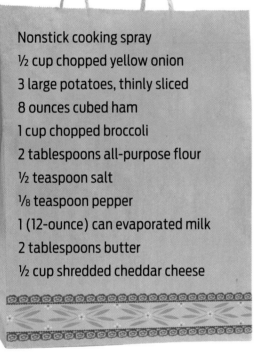

Nonstick cooking spray

½ cup chopped yellow onion

3 large potatoes, thinly sliced

8 ounces cubed ham

1 cup chopped broccoli

2 tablespoons all-purpose flour

½ teaspoon salt

⅛ teaspoon pepper

1 (12-ounce) can evaporated milk

2 tablespoons butter

½ cup shredded cheddar cheese

1. Preheat oven to 325 degrees. Spray a 1.5-quart temp-tations® dish with nonstick cooking spray.

2. In a nonstick skillet, over medium heat, cook the onion until translucent, about 5 minutes.

3. Place half of the sliced potatoes in the prepared dish and top with the onion. Top onions with ham and broccoli.

4. Whisk the flour, salt, and pepper into the evaporated milk, and pour half of the flour mixture over the ham mixture. Layer the remaining potato slices over the broccoli, and top with remaining evaporated milk.

5. Drizzle melted butter over casserole, cover with aluminum foil, and bake 1 hour.

6. Remove aluminum foil, sprinkle with cheddar cheese, and bake until potatoes are tender, 30 minutes. Let cool 5 minutes before serving.

TARA'S TRADITIONS *My family loves this dish. Sometimes Mom adds macaroni to it for a little texture.*

Seafood

PREP TIME: 10 mins   **COOK TIME: 30 mins**   **SERVES: 4**   **LID-IT®**

Crab Cakes by Tara®

I love crab cakes, simple as that! Crab cakes are a comfort food and eaten any time of the day…breakfast, lunch, as an appetizer, or as a simple seafood entrée. Crab cakes served with a light salad or rice dish make a wonderful meal and can also be a sumptuous starter.

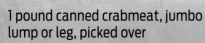

1 pound canned crabmeat, jumbo lump or leg, picked over

½ cup mayonnaise, divided

1¼ teaspoons Old Bay seasoning

1 tablespoon Dijon mustard

¼ cup minced scallions (about 4 scallions)

2 tablespoons beaten egg (from 1 large egg)

2 tablespoons unseasoned bread crumbs

1 teaspoon finely grated lemon zest and 2 teaspoons fresh lemon juice (from 1 lemon)

canola oil or spray

1. Preheat oven to 425 degrees. Drain crabmeat over a colander, pressing gently to extract liquid.

2. In a large bowl, combine ¼ cup mayonnaise, Old Bay, mustard, scallions, and egg. Gently fold in crabmeat and bread crumbs to combine.

3. Shape crab mixture into four 4-ounce, 1-inch-thick cakes.

4. Bake on temp-tations® Lid-it®, until cooked through and golden brown, flipping cakes and rotating pan halfway through, 20 minutes.

5. Meanwhile, make lemon mayonnaise: In a small bowl combine remaining mayonnaise, lemon zest, and lemon juice. Stir to combine. Serve crab cakes warm with lemon mayonnaise.

SEAFOOD

TARA'S TIDBITS™ *Fresh crabmeat can be substituted when available. The key to light crab cakes is not going overboard on the bread crumbs. Starting with well-drained crab will ensure light and fluffy cakes with prominent crab flavor.*

Baked Asian Salmon

Take an upstream trip on the Orient Express for the most moist and flavorful salmon you've ever tasted. Using your Lid-it® to cover your temp-tations® presentable ovenware™ makes steaming simple and takes all the work out of using a steamer or boiling water.

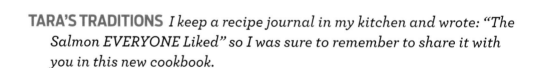

4 tablespoons soy sauce

3 tablespoons rice vinegar

1 tablespoon sugar

2 teaspoons powdered ginger

1 clove garlic, peeled and thinly sliced

1 teaspoon sesame oil

4 (6-ounce) salmon fillets, skinned

3 scallions, halved lengthwise and cut into 2-inch pieces

freshly ground pepper

2 cups steamed white rice for serving

1. Preheat oven to 375 degrees.

2. In a 4-quart temp-tations® dish, combine soy sauce, rice vinegar, sugar, ginger, garlic, and sesame oil. Stir to dissolve sugar.

3. Score the salmon lightly on skinned side. Add salmon to the sauce, turning once to coat, and place scored side down. Top the salmon with scallions and season with freshly ground pepper.

4. Cover dish with temp-tations® Lid-it® and cook until salmon is just cooked through, about 12 to 15 minutes. Spoon sauce over salmon and serve with rice.

TARA'S TRADITIONS *I keep a recipe journal in my kitchen and wrote: "The Salmon EVERYONE Liked" so I was sure to remember to share it with you in this new cookbook.*

SEAFOOD

Fire Cracker Tilapia

Flaky, mild-mannered tilapia falls apart to the touch and melts in your mouth. This recipe is a cinch to make and not only comes together quickly but bakes in a matter of minutes. It's a good dish to prepare for someone who is on the fence about fish or just a picky eater.

½ teaspoon kosher salt

2 teaspoons chili powder, divided

½ teaspoon dried oregano

2 large eggs

2 tablespoons tomato paste

2½ teaspoons prepared horseradish

2 cups crushed butter cracker crumbs (such as Ritz Crackers)

2 tablespoons olive oil

1½ pounds (4 fillets) tilapia, halved lengthwise into 8 pieces

1 lime, cut into wedges for serving

1. Preheat oven to 450 degrees.

2. In a small bowl combine ½ teaspoon salt, 1 teaspoon chili powder, and oregano.

3. In a shallow bowl whisk together eggs, tomato paste, and horseradish; set aside. In a second shallow bowl combine cracker crumbs, olive oil, and remaining 1 teaspoon chili powder.

4. Sprinkle tilapia with chili powder mixture, then dip in egg mixture, letting excess drip off, then dip fish in cracker crumbs on both sides to coat. Place on temp-tations® Lid-it®. Repeat with remaining fillets.

5. Bake until crust is golden and tilapia is cooked, rotating halfway through and flipping each piece, 15 minutes. Serve with lime wedges.

SEAFOOD

TARA'S TIDBITS™ *Substitute chipotle chili powder if you have it for an awesome smoked flavor. It's fun for the little ones to crunch up the butter crackers to make the crust, and the familiar crackers and the non-fishy flavor make this a great dish for introducing kids to fish.*

PREP TIME: 15 mins

COOK TIME: 30 mins

SERVES: 4

temp·tations.
PRESENTABLE OVENWARE
by Tara

4 QUART

Panko Fish and Chips

I love fish and chips. This is a more streamlined, more healthful fish and chips recipe. It's oven-baked and coated with crunchy panko crumbs. Mom introduced me to panko and it's delicious. This is a quick and simple way to make this dish.

cooking spray

2 baking potatoes, scrubbed and cut into ¾-inch-thick wedges

2 tablespoons olive oil

1 large egg

1 tablespoon water

1¼ cups plain panko bread crumbs

2 tablespoons chopped fresh flat-leaf Italian parsley

¾ teaspoon dried thyme

1¼ pounds cod fillets, bones removed, cut diagonally into 1-inch-wide strips

2 tablespoons Dijon mustard

½ teaspoon salt

¼ teaspoon cracked black pepper

lemon wedges, tartar sauce, and malt vinegar for garnish

1. Preheat oven to 400 degrees. Spray temp-tations® 4-quart dish and large temp-tations® Lid-it® with cooking spray.

2. Place potato wedges in 4-quart dish with olive oil and toss to coat. Bake until tender, stirring twice, 20 to 25 minutes. Meanwhile, in a shallow dish, beat together egg and water. On waxed paper, combine bread crumbs, parsley, and thyme.

3. Brush fish pieces on both sides with mustard. Dip each piece of fish in egg mixture, letting the excess egg mixture drip off back into the dish. Then dip each piece of fish into bread-crumb mixture to coat.

4. Arrange fish pieces in a single layer on Lid-it®. Place fish in oven with potato wedges and bake until fish turns opaque and potatoes are tender, 15 minutes.

5. To serve, arrange fish pieces on one side of Lid-it®. Toss potato wedges with salt and cracked black pepper. Place potato wedges on Lid-it® with the fish. Garnish with lemon wedges, tartar sauce, and malt vinegar.

SEAFOOD

TARA'S TIDBITS™ *Panko are Japanese-style bread crumbs and should be easily found at your local grocery store.*

Baked "Fried" Shrimp

Better than takeout and also healthier. It's family- and kid-friendly, and no one will guess that it's not fried.

SEAFOOD

canola oil for dish

½ cup all-purpose flour

kosher salt and freshly ground black pepper

1 large egg, lightly beaten

3 cups cornflakes

¾ pound large shrimp (about 16 shrimp), peeled, deveined, tails attached

½ cup apricot preserves

1 tablespoon white vinegar

2 tablespoons Dijon mustard

2 teaspoons soy sauce

1. Preheat oven to 375 degrees. Lightly coat a 4-quart temp-tations® dish with oil and set aside.

2. In a shallow bowl, season the flour with 1 teaspoon salt and ½ teaspoon pepper. Pour the egg into a separate shallow bowl.

3. Place the cornflakes in a large resealable plastic bag. Use a rolling pin or your hands to crush the cornflakes into coarse crumbs. Transfer the crumbs to a shallow bowl.

4. Dip each shrimp into the flour mixture, then into the eggs, and then into the cornflakes, turning to coat. Transfer the shrimp to prepared dish. Bake until golden brown, crispy, and cooked through, 15 to 20 minutes.

5. Meanwhile, in a 6-ounce dish, microwave the apricot preserves until warm, about 45 seconds. Add the vinegar, mustard, and soy sauce and mix to combine. Serve the shrimp warm with the dipping sauce.

TARA'S TRADITIONS *Since the "secret" ingredient in this recipe is a big bunch of cornflakes I think it definitely qualifies for one of my backward banquet dishes!*

PREP TIME: 5 mins

COOK TIME: 20 mins

SERVES: 4

temp·tations
PRESENTABLE OVENWARE
by Tara
2.5 QUART

Bimbi's Baked Salmon with Yogurt Dill Sauce

This is the "go-to" recipe for fish—it's so easy, it should be illegal. It's an elegant dish and I love it best on hot summery days served with fresh steamed asparagus and corn on the cob.

4 (4- to 6-ounce) fresh boneless, skinless salmon fillets

2 tablespoons extra-virgin olive oil

kosher salt and freshly ground black pepper

½ cup plain yogurt

2 tablespoons fresh chopped dill, plus dill springs for serving

1 clove garlic, minced

2 teaspoons fresh lemon zest

1 tablespoon fresh lemon juice

1. Preheat oven to 400 degrees.

2. Brush the salmon fillets all over with olive oil, season with ½ teaspoon salt and ¼ teaspoon pepper, and place in a 2.5-quart temp-tations® dish.

3. Bake until cooked through but still moist, 15 to 20 minutes.

4. Meanwhile, in a medium bowl mix the yogurt, dill, garlic, lemon zest, lemon juice, ¼ teaspoon salt, and ¼ teaspoon pepper until combined. Drizzle the sauce over the salmon and garnish each piece with a sprig of dill, if desired. Serve with rice and vegetables.

TARA'S TIDBITS™ *I'm always glad when there are leftovers. It's great over a green salad or even between two slices of pumpernickel bread. It's also as good cold or at room temperature as it is served hot.*

SEAFOOD

PREP TIME: 15 mins

COOK TIME: 15 mins

SERVES: 4

temp-tations.
PRESENTABLE OVENWARE
by Tara
4 QUART

Tasty Fish Tacos

These tacos will make you want to hug somebody, they're so darn good. Keep 'em coming for walk-in friends and neighbors. Great summer back-yard dinner—walk in the door at 5:17, and dinner is on the table in 30 min-utes. If you prepare everything in the morning, dinner can be in 15 minutes!

1 pound firm mild white fish, such as tilapia or halibut, cut into 3-inch pieces

1 tablespoon extra-virgin olive oil

kosher salt and freshly ground black pepper

2 tablespoons fresh lime juice

½ cup sour cream

8 (6-inch) corn tortillas

2 cups green cabbage, shredded

4 radishes, thinly sliced

1 medium tomato, chopped

SEAFOOD

1. Preheat the oven to 375 degrees. Place the fish in a 4-quart temp-tations® dish. Brush the fish with olive oil and season with ½ teaspoon salt and ¼ teaspoon pepper.

2. Bake until the fish is cooked through, 10 to 15 minutes.

3. Meanwhile, combine the lime juice, sour cream, and 1 teaspoon salt in a 6-ounce dipping dish and stir to combine. Set aside.

4. Wrap the tortillas between two paper towels and microwave on high until pliable, about 30 seconds. Top each tortilla with a piece of fish, cabbage, radish, and tomato and drizzle with the sour cream sauce.

TARA'S TIDBITS™ *Serve with a basket of tortilla chips and it's real easy to find guacamole in the refrigerator section of your grocery store. Some salsa on the side and you're all set.*

PREP TIME: 15 mins

COOK TIME: 35 mins

SERVES: 4

temp-tations.
PRESENTABLE OVENWARE
by tara
LID-IT®

Crispy Shrimp Rolls

These are amazingly addictive and highly recommended. They're easy to customize by adding any of your preferred veggies, or raisins for sweetness. You can always double the recipe and make more than enough for a crowd.

SEAFOOD

1 tablespoon sesame oil

1 teaspoon sugar

1 egg white, lightly beaten

½ teaspoon kosher salt

¼ teaspoon freshly ground pepper

6 ounces ground pork

6 ounces medium shrimp, peeled and deveined, coarsely chopped

3 scallions, light and dark green parts, thinly sliced

4 spring roll or wonton wrappers, cut in half diagonally

1 tablespoon vegetable oil

¼ cup sweet chili sauce or duck sauce for dipping

1. Preheat oven with a temp-tations® Lid-it® to 425 degrees. Set aside a small bowl of cold water.

2. In a large bowl whisk the sesame oil, sugar, egg white, salt, and pepper until combined. Fold in pork, shrimp, and scallions, stirring until combined.

3. Lay four spring roll triangle halves out on a cutting board with the pointed end facing away. Place scant 3 tablespoons of filling toward the cut end of the spring roll, fold corners in, and roll toward pointed end (rolling away from you). Wet end of wrapper with water and seal.

4. Repeat with remaining wrappers and filling. Brush spring rolls with vegetable oil and transfer to preheated temp-tations® Lid-it®.

5. Bake until golden and crisp, about 18 minutes. Serve warm with sweet chili or duck sauce.

TARA'S TIDBITS™ *Covering the completed spring rolls with a slightly damp paper towel prevents dough from drying out. They freeze well for reheating later.*

Pasta, Rice, & Bread

Prep Time: 30 mins

 COOKING TIME: 80 mins

SERVES: 6

 temp·tations
PRESENTABLE OVENWARE
by Tara™

4 QUART

Caramelized Onion Tart

This is a very simple side dish and perfect for that Sunday brunch or when having guests stay in your home. It keeps really well in the fridge if you have any left, and with temp-tations®, reheating it is a breeze!

2 tablespoons olive oil

2 tablespoons unsalted butter

2 large onions, halved and cut into ¼-inch half moons

kosher salt to taste

3 tablespoons thyme, plus two sprigs for garnish

1 sheet puff pastry, defrosted

1 egg white

½ cup grated Gruyère cheese

1. Preheat oven to 400 degrees.

2. In a large skillet over medium heat, combine olive oil and butter. When the butter has melted add the onions and stir to coat. Spread the onions evenly to cover the bottom of the pan, cook 10 minutes, and then season with salt. Reduce heat if the onions begin to burn. Continue cooking until the onions are deep brown and lacquered, 30 minutes. Stir in the thyme.

3. Meanwhile, generously flour a work surface and rolling pin. Roll the puff pastry out to a 9½-inch by 13-inch rectangle. Brush the pastry with the egg white. Using a very sharp knife, trim away 1-inch from each edge. Place the trimmed strips onto the pastry to create a raised rim. Transfer the pastry to a 4-quart temp-tations® dish.

4. Using a fork, pierce the pastry all over the inside of crust the raised rim. Bake until puffed and golden, 15 to 20 minutes. Scatter the Gruyère all over the tart. Spoon the onions over, covering the interior of the tart. Return to the oven and bake until the cheese melts, about 15 to 20 minutes. Garnish with the thyme and serve.

5. Scatter the Gruyère all over the tart. Spoon the onions over, covering the interior of the tart. Return to the oven and bake until the cheese melts, about 15 to 20 minutes. Garnish with the thyme and serve.

TARA'S TIDBITS™ *Just remember, the more thyme the better! Think of this as a deconstructed French onion soup.*

 PREP TIME: 10 mins

 COOK TIME: 30 mins

 SERVES: 8

 temp-tations.
PRESENTABLE OVENWARE
by Tara

4 QUART

Orecchiette Margherita

This is a great pasta dish, a Mediterranean-style family staple and one that's been handed down in my family and now, on to yours!

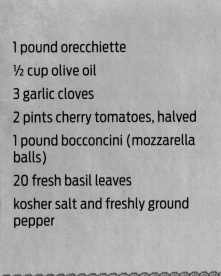

1 pound orecchiette

½ cup olive oil

3 garlic cloves

2 pints cherry tomatoes, halved

1 pound bocconcini (mozzarella balls)

20 fresh basil leaves

kosher salt and freshly ground pepper

1. Cook the orecchiette according to package directions.

2. Meanwhile in a medium saucepan over medium heat add the olive oil and heat until hot but not smoking, then add the garlic and cook until fragrant and soft, 2 to 3 minutes. Remove from heat and set aside.

3. With a slotted spoon, transfer the pasta to a temp-tations® 4-quart dish.

4. Add the tomatoes and the bocconcini to the pasta. Pour the hot oil and garlic over the pasta and stir to thoroughly combine. Add the basil leaves and stir. Season with the salt and pepper; serve warm.

TARA'S TRADITIONS *I make a modified version several times a month and add whatever's fresh (like yellow squash and zucchini) and if I really want to "pig out"...bacon! Let's face it; usually everything tastes better with bacon.*

Orzo, Shrimp, Tomato, and Feta Casserole

This is a great everyday dish! It will certainly impress your guests, and yourself! It's very satisfying and a good choice when cooking for a crowd.

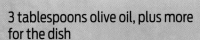

3 tablespoons olive oil, plus more for the dish

1 medium onion, finely chopped

1 red bell pepper, cored, seeded, and roughly chopped

2 garlic cloves, minced

1 teaspoon dried oregano

¼ teaspoon dried hot red pepper flakes

½ cup white wine

1 (28-ounce) can crushed tomatoes

kosher salt, to taste

2 pounds large shrimp, shelled and deveined

1 cup frozen peas (optional)

1 pound orzo (rice-shaped pasta)

1 pound feta, patted dry and crumbled

1. Preheat oven to 425 degrees. Grease a temp-tations® 4-quart dish with olive oil.

2. In a large skillet, heat 1 tablespoon of the oil over medium-high heat. Add the onion, pepper, garlic, oregano, and hot red pepper flakes and cook, stirring, until fragrant and the onions and peppers are softened, 3 to 4 minutes. Add the wine and boil until the liquid is reduced by half.

3. Stir in the tomatoes and salt, reduce heat, and simmer, stirring, until the sauce thickens slightly, 8 to 10 minutes. Add the shrimp and heat until just cooked through, about 3 minutes. Add the peas, if using, and stir to combine.

4. Meanwhile, bring a 6-quart pot of salted water to a boil. Cook the orzo until firm to the bite. Reserve ½ cup of the cooking water and drain the orzo. Return the orzo to the pot; toss with the remaining 2 tablespoons of olive oil. Stir in the sauce and cooking water. Season to taste.

5. Spoon half of the pasta into the prepared temp-tations® dish. Sprinkle half of the feta over it. Top with remaining pasta and feta. Bake until the cheese is just melted and the orzo is heated through, 15 to 20 minutes.

TARA'S TIDBITS™ *I always encourage you to prepare ahead! You can prepare this dish the night before, but don't bake it. Pull it out of the fridge, let it get to room temperature, then bake until it starts to turn brown.*

Game Day Bowties with Sausage and Broccoli

A really good, quick pasta dish. I cooked this for a football party and everyone loved it!

4 links sweet Italian sausage, casings removed

1 head (2 pounds) broccoli, cut into florets

1 pound farfalle or other short, shaped pasta

½ teaspoon hot red pepper flakes

kosher salt and freshly ground pepper to taste

½ cup grated parmesan, plus more for serving

1. Bring a 6-quart pot of salted water to a boil.

2. Meanwhile, in a large skillet, over medium-high heat, add the sausage and cook, breaking up the meat with a wooden spoon. When the meat has lost all of its pink color, remove from the heat.

3. Drop the broccoli into the boiling water and cook until fork tender, 4 to 6 minutes. Remove with a slotted spoon to a separate bowl. Bring the water back to a boil and cook the pasta according to package instructions.

4. Transfer the cooked pasta to the skillet using a slotted spoon. Return sausage mixture to medium heat and stir to thoroughly combine. Add more pasta water, as needed, to moisten the pasta. Season with the red pepper flakes, salt, and pepper. Stir in the grated parmesan, transfer to a temp-tations® 4-quart dish, and serve with extra parmesan on the side.

PASTA, RICE, & BREAD

TARA'S TIDBITS™ *You can always substitute chicken or turkey sausage to lighten it up just a bit. "Farfalle" is the Italian name for "bowtie" pasta.*

PREP TIME: 8 mins

COOK TIME: 20 mins

SERVES: 4

temp-tations.
PRESENTABLE OVENWARE
by Tara
1 QUART

Mo' Rockin' Casserole

This is a very welcome change from your average pasta or rice dishes. It's light and subtle, sweet and nutty, and very easy to make.

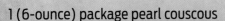

1 (6-ounce) package pearl couscous

1 tablespoon plus 1 teaspoon red wine vinegar

2 teaspoons honey

½ teaspoon kosher salt

¼ teaspoon fresh ground pepper

4 tablespoons extra-virgin olive oil

⅓ cup peeled and thinly sliced red onion

2 tablespoons chopped fresh parsley

¼ cup sliced dried apricots (5 dried apricots)

½ cup dried cranberries (or Craisins)

¼ cup sliced almonds, toasted

1. Cook couscous according to package instructions. Alternatively: In a medium saucepan, over medium-high heat, bring 2½ cups water to a boil, add couscous, stir once, and cook uncovered until water is mostly absorbed, 12 minutes. Cover and let stand 5 minutes.

2. Meanwhile, in a 1-quart temp-tations® dish, whisk together red wine vinegar, honey, salt, and pepper. Whisk in olive oil in a slow stream. Add onions, stirring to coat. Set aside.

3. Drain couscous and add to bowl with dressing. Add parsley, apricots, dried cranberries, and toasted almonds; stir to combine. Adjust seasoning to taste. Serve immediately.

PASTA, RICE, & BREAD

TARA'S TIDBITS™ *I like to add some roasted chicken to this dish or just eat it alongside whatever main dish you're having that night, like lamb or beef.*

PREP TIME: 15 mins

COOK TIME: 40 mins

SERVES 4

temp-tations.
PRESENTABLE OVENWARE
by Tara

PIE PLATE

Spaghetti Pie

This is one of those no-brainers my family always enjoyed; the best part is you can cook the spaghetti fresh or use leftovers!

nonstick cooking spray

½ pound spaghetti (dry or cooked)

1 tablespoon olive oil

1 medium onion (8 ounces), chopped

1 medium zucchini (7 ounces), cut into ½-inch pieces

1 pound lean ground beef

1 teaspoon Italian seasoning

½ teaspoon salt

¼ teaspoon pepper

2 cups store-bought pasta sauce

1¾ cups shredded four-cheese Italian blend, divided

2 tablespoons chopped flat-leaf parsley, optional

1. Preheat oven to 350 degrees. Spray temptations® 9-inch pie plate with cooking spray.

2. If using fresh spaghetti, prepare according package directions; drain and set aside.

3. Meanwhile, in 12-inch skillet over medium-high heat, heat olive oil and cook onion, stirring occasionally, 3 minutes. Add zucchini and cook, stirring occasionally, 8 minutes. Add ground beef, Italian seasoning, salt, and pepper and cook until beef is browned and cooked through and vegetables are tender, 8 minutes.

4. Add pasta sauce and spaghetti. Cook until heated through, then stir in 1 cup Italian cheese blend.

5. Spoon spaghetti mixture into pie plate. Sprinkle with remaining ¾ cup Italian cheese blend. Bake until bubbly and heated through, 20 to 30 minutes. Sprinkle with chopped parsley, if desired.

PASTA, RICE, & BREAD

TARA'S TIDBITS™ *This recipe is perfect for the end of the week when you don't have a lot of groceries in the fridge. It's a great potluck dish to take along to a party or any gathering!*

Phyllo Dough Spinach Pie

I always knew spinach tasted good, but not this good! It's always the hit of the party and one of the more healthy options on the table. I promise, if you're bringing this somewhere, it will be the first to go.

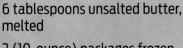

6 tablespoons unsalted butter, melted

2 (10-ounce) packages frozen chopped spinach, thawed

1½ cups ricotta cheese

1 cup crumbled feta cheese

2 large eggs

kosher salt and freshly ground black pepper

pinch of nutmeg

16 sheets phyllo dough, from 1 (16-ounce) package

1. Preheat the oven to 350 degrees. Lightly brush a 4-quart temp-tations® dish with some of the melted butter.

2. Place the spinach in a dishtowel and wring out excess liquid until spinach is dry.

3. In a large bowl, add the spinach, ricotta, feta, eggs, ½ teaspoon salt, ¼ teaspoon pepper, and a pinch of nutmeg and stir until combined.

4. Working piece by piece, brush 8 sheets of phyllo dough with melted butter, layering them individually, as they are buttered, into the prepared temp-tations® dish. Spread the spinach mixture on top, and top with the remaining buttered 8 sheets of phyllo dough. Tuck the edges of the phyllo dough into the dish.

5. Bake until golden brown, 45 to 50 minutes. Cool 10 minutes before serving.

TARA'S TRADITIONS *This is a great way to get your kids to eat spinach. Amy calls this dish the "Popeye Sandwich"!*

PASTA, RICE, & BREAD

Country Bread Casserole

This dish can easily be transformed into a delicious vegetarian recipe. Simply add an extra 2 cups of spinach in place of the ham, and you'll be ready to feed all the herbivores in your house!

extra-virgin olive oil for baking pan

1 (16-ounce) day-old country bread loaf, sliced ¼-inch thick

1 cup prepared pasta sauce

6 ounces Gruyère cheese, grated (2 cups)

4 ounces thinly sliced deli ham

4 cups baby spinach

1½ cups low-sodium chicken or vegetable broth

1. Preheat oven to 400 degrees. Lightly brush a 2.5-quart temp-tations® dish with oil.

2. Line the bottom of the dish with 4 to 5 slices of bread. Cut slices in half to fit snugly, if necessary.

3. Spread ½ cup pasta sauce onto the bread, top with ½ cup gruyere cheese, then 2 ounces ham and 2 cups spinach. Repeat—layering, in order: bread, sauce, cheese, ham, and spinach—and ending with a final layer of bread. If necessary, press down to compact the ingredients to fit in the dish.

4. Pour the chicken broth over the casserole. Cover with aluminum foil.

5. Bake for 30 minutes. Uncover and spread the remaining 1 cup cheese over the top. Return to the oven and bake, uncovered, until the liquid is absorbed and reduced, and the cheese has melted and browned, 25 to 30 minutes. Let cool slightly before serving.

PASTA, RICE, & BREAD

TARA'S TRADITIONS *I especially love this one because it's a cross between the old-fashioned Italian deep-dish pizza I loved from the festivals in Little Italy and the French Monte Cristo sandwich I remember from a restaurant I loved in New York City.*

PREP TIME: 15 mins

COOK TIME: 40 mins

SERVES: 6

temp-tations.
PRESENTABLE OVENWARE
by Tara
2.5 QUART

Mac 'n Cheese with Sausage & Peas Please

Decadent, that's all I have to say. This is not your typical shells and cheese recipe; by adding in the sausage and peas it steps this dish up from average to exceptional!

3 tablespoons unsalted butter, divided, plus more for dish

12 ounces dried macaroni pasta or other small shaped pasta

8 ounces sausage, casings removed

3 tablespoons all-purpose flour

2 cups whole milk

10 ounces sharp white cheddar cheese, grated (3½ cups)

kosher salt and freshly ground black pepper

1 cup (5 ounces) frozen peas

¼ cup bread crumbs

1. Preheat oven to 400 degrees. Lightly coat a 2.5-quart temp-tations® dish with butter. Bring a large pot of salted water to a boil and cook the pasta according to package instructions. Drain and return to the pot.

2. Meanwhile, in a medium saucepan over medium-high heat, melt 1½ tablespoons of butter. Add the sausage and cook, breaking meat with a wooden spoon, until cooked through and crumbled, about 4 minutes.

3. Add the remaining butter and flour to the sausage, stirring constantly until coated. Add the milk, whisking constantly until boiling and thickened. Off heat, stir in the cheese, 1 teaspoon salt, ½ teaspoon pepper, and peas; cook until cheese is melted and smooth.

4. Add the cheese mixture to the pasta and toss to coat. Pour into the prepared temp-tations® dish and top with the bread crumbs.

5. Bake until golden brown on top and the cheese is bubbly, 40 minutes. Serve immediately.

TARA'S TIDBITS™ *Easily doubled for a potluck. Your bread crumbs can be either white or Italian, whichever are your favorite; and the same with the pasta. You can also try smoked sausage as an option for a little more kick, or turkey sausage for a healthier twist.*

PASTA, RICE, & BREAD

Cherry Tomato and Pesto Tart

If you want to impress, make this for a party—it will easily serve a dozen guests. It disappears, and is super-easy to make!

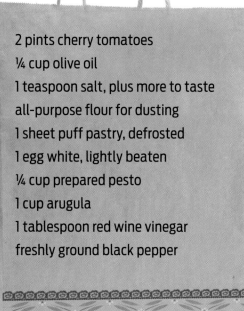

2 pints cherry tomatoes

¼ cup olive oil

1 teaspoon salt, plus more to taste

all-purpose flour for dusting

1 sheet puff pastry, defrosted

1 egg white, lightly beaten

¼ cup prepared pesto

1 cup arugula

1 tablespoon red wine vinegar

freshly ground black pepper

1. Preheat the oven to 350 degrees. Arrange the tomatoes in a single layer on a baking sheet. Pour the olive oil over and toss to coat. Season with salt and bake until the tomatoes begin to shrink, about 45 minutes.

2. Meanwhile, generously flour a work surface and rolling pin. Roll the pastry sheet out to a 9½ by 11-inch rectangle. Brush the pastry with the egg white. Using a very sharp knife, trim away 1 inch from each edge. Place the trimmed strips onto the pastry to create a raised rim.

3. Transfer the pastry to a temp-tations® Lid-it®. Using a fork, pierce the pastry all over inside the raised rim. Bake until puffed and golden, 15 to 20 minutes.

4. Spread the interior of the pastry with the pesto. Arrange the tomatoes over the pastry in a single layer. Return the tart to the oven and bake 5 to 10 minutes more.

5. Meanwhile, toss the arugula with the olive oil and red wine vinegar. Season with salt and pepper. Arrange over the tomatoes in a pile in the center. Serve immediately.

TARA'S TIDBITS™ *Sausage or bacon added on top turns this delicious tart into a hearty meal.*

PASTA, RICE, & BREAD

Sides

Fried Pickles

I'm addicted to these fried pickles and had the pleasure of eating these in college. The South is invited into my Pennsylvania kitchen anytime!

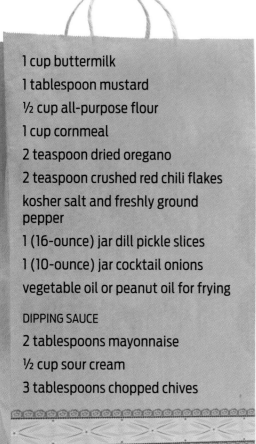

1 cup buttermilk

1 tablespoon mustard

½ cup all-purpose flour

1 cup cornmeal

2 teaspoon dried oregano

2 teaspoon crushed red chili flakes

kosher salt and freshly ground pepper

1 (16-ounce) jar dill pickle slices

1 (10-ounce) jar cocktail onions

vegetable oil or peanut oil for frying

DIPPING SAUCE

2 tablespoons mayonnaise

½ cup sour cream

3 tablespoons chopped chives

1. Preheat oven to 350 degrees with rack in the center.

2. In a large bowl, mix buttermilk and mustard.

3. In a shallow dish, mix flour, cornmeal, dried oregano, crushed red chili flakes, salt, and pepper.

4. Drain the jar of dill pickle slices and the jar of cocktail onions. Mix pickles in buttermilk mixture. Roll in flour mix.

5. Bake in a 4-quart temp-tations® dish until pickles are golden brown and crispy, 15 minutes.

6. Make dipping sauce: in a small bowl, combine mayonnaise, sour cream, and chopped chives. Serve with warm fried pickles.

TARA'S TRADITIONS *The familiar Southern favorite fried pickles made easy—and lighter in calories—by oven baking with temp-tations®. Pearl onions and chili add a nice little kick. I learned to cook Southern from Mom. She learned from a sergeant's wife who lived across the street from my parents when Dad was in the army on the West Coast.*

SIDES

Baked Beans

This is a great recipe! I make this on the fly because I always have these ingredients on hand. It's great to add baked beans as another side dish to almost any meal.

2 cups navy beans (or canned navy beans, drained and rinsed)

4 tablespoons molasses

¾ cup ketchup

2 tablespoons spicy brown mustard

2 tablespoons Worcestershire sauce

2 tablespoons light brown sugar

pinch kosher salt and ground pepper

1 large onion, finely diced

8 ounces slab bacon (rind removed), cut into small cubes

5 cups water

1. Soak beans overnight in enough cold water to cover by 1 inch.

2. Drain and place in a temp-tations® 3-quart dish.

3. Preheat oven to 350 degrees.

4. In a small saucepan over medium heat, bring the molasses, ketchup, mustard, Worcestershire sauce, sugar, and salt and pepper to a boil. Remove from heat and add molasses mixture to the beans along with the onion, bacon, beans, and water.

5. Transfer to oven, stir well, and bake, stirring occasionally, adding more water if necessary, until the beans are tender, about 4 hours. When beans are tender, bake uncovered until sauce is thickened, 20 minutes.

TARA'S TIDBITS™ *For an easy and filling weeknight supper, try these beans poured over a baked potato topped with sour cream. If you're serving as a side, serve with tortilla chips!*

SIDES

PREP TIME: 10 mins

COOK TIME: 40 mins

SERVES: 8

temp-tations
PRESENTABLE OVENWARE
by Tara
2 QUART

Mom's Succotash

This is one of our favorite family traditions. I've tasted many versions over the years, and without a doubt Mom's is the best. It's colorful and looks beautiful on the table, and it's filling enough for a meal!

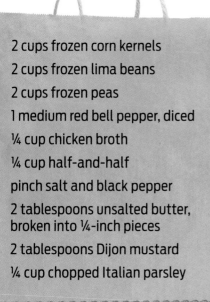

2 cups frozen corn kernels

2 cups frozen lima beans

2 cups frozen peas

1 medium red bell pepper, diced

¼ cup chicken broth

¼ cup half-and-half

pinch salt and black pepper

2 tablespoons unsalted butter, broken into ¼-inch pieces

2 tablespoons Dijon mustard

¼ cup chopped Italian parsley

1. Preheat the oven to 400 degrees.

2. In a 2-quart temp-tations® dish, combine the corn, lima beans, peas, and bell peppers. Add the chicken broth, half-and-half, salt, and pepper, stirring to combine. Top with butter.

3. Cover and bake until vegetables are tender, stirring occasionally, 40 minutes.

4. Add Dijon mustard and chopped parsley, stirring well to combine. Serve warm.

TARA'S TRADITIONS *This is a super-easy way of cooking frozen vegetables right out of the freezer. If you care to, substitute fresh or canned veggies—just reduce the cooking time accordingly. Mom knows most of us never cared for lima beans when we were young so she often substituted edamame. Try that!*

SIDES

PREP TIME: 15 mins

COOK TIME: 30 mins

SERVES: 8

3 QUART

Cauliflower Gratin

For those of you who aren't cauliflower fans, you'll love this! Easily a holiday showstopper, this recipe is simple enough to make on a weeknight for the family.

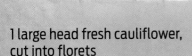

1 large head fresh cauliflower, cut into florets

¾ cup chopped cured ham

5 tablespoons unsalted butter, plus more for dish

4 tablespoons all-purpose flour

4 cups milk

2 teaspoons fresh thyme (or 1 teaspoon dried thyme)

1 teaspoon salt

¼ teaspoon fresh grated nutmeg (or 1 teaspoon powdered nutmeg)

1½ cups grated Gruyère cheese

½ cup dry seasoned bread crumbs

1 teaspoon freshly ground pepper

1. Preheat oven to 375 degrees. Butter a 3-quart temp-tations® dish and set aside.

2. In a large pot of boiling water fitted with a steamer basket, steam the cauliflower florets until fork tender, 7 to 9 minutes. Drain and rinse in cold water. Arrange in a single layer in the prepared dish. Add the ham and toss to combine.

3. In a large saucepan over medium-high heat, melt the butter and whisk in the flour. Cook, whisking for 2 minutes. Gradually add the milk, whisking continuously, until the sauce thickens and is heated through.

4. Remove from the heat and add the thyme, salt, and nutmeg. Pour the sauce over the cauliflower and toss to thoroughly coat each floret.

5. Bake the gratin for 15 minutes. Combine the Gruyère and bread crumbs and sprinkle over the cauliflower. Bake until the cheese is melted and the bread crumbs are golden, about 15 minutes. Season with pepper and serve.

SIDES

TARA'S TIDBITS™ *I recommend serving with pork or lamb chops for a guaranteed slam dunk! I also love the simple white color of this recipe.*

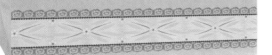

 PREP TIME: 30 mins

 COOK TIME: 1 hour

 SERVES: 6

 temp-tations
PRESENTABLE OVENWARE
by tara
LID-IT®

Butternut Squash Tart

"OMG"—this one is a serious threat to my traditional pumpkin pie!

2 large eggs

1 sheet frozen puff pastry, thawed

2 medium butternut squash, peeled and cut into ¼-inch half-circles

1 tablespoon olive oil

3 shallots, thinly sliced (or 1 small onion)

1 pound fresh ricotta cheese

1 tablespoon heavy cream

kosher salt and fresh ground pepper

1 tablespoon thyme leaves (or ¼ teaspoon dried thyme)

1 tablespoon sage, finely chopped (or ¼ teaspoon dried sage)

4 ounces pancetta, very thinly sliced into 1-inch pieces (or bacon)

1. Preheat oven to 400 degrees.

2. Separate one of the eggs and beat the white in a small bowl. Generously flour a work surface and rolling pin. Roll the puff pastry sheet out to a 9½ by 11-inch rectangle. Brush with the egg white. Using a very sharp knife, trim away 1 inch from each edge. Place the trimmed strips onto the pastry to create a raised rim. Transfer the pastry to a temp-tations® Lid-it®. Pierce the pastry with a fork all over inside the raised rim. Chill in the refrigerator for 30 minutes.

3. Meanwhile, toss the squash slices in the olive oil, spread on a baking sheet, and roast about 7 minutes. Add the shallots to the squash, tossing to coat, and bake until the squash is tender but not falling apart, about 8 minutes more.

4. In a medium bowl, combine the ricotta, remaining egg, and heavy cream. Season with salt and pepper; set aside.

5. Reduce the oven heat to 375 degrees. Bake the pastry sheet until lightly golden, about 10 minutes. Remove from the oven and spread the ricotta filling within its borders. Scatter the squash, shallots, sage, and thyme over it and bake until the pastry is golden brown, about 25 minutes. Top with the pancetta and serve.

TARA'S TIDBITS™ *Personally, I like my butternut squash cheesy. If you feel the same way, don't hesitate to spread ½ cup of grated parmesan cheese when you add the ricotta filling in step 3.*

SIDES

PREP TIME: 10 mins

COOK TIME: 45 mins

SERVES: 6

temp·tations
PRESENTABLE OVENWARE
by tara

4 QUART

Tara's White Bean Salad with Roasted Cherry Tomatoes

It's simple, popular, colorful, and healthy, and a great dish to take to picnics and cookouts. It's nutritious, delicious, and so refreshing!

2 pints cherry tomatoes

¼ cup olive oil

kosher salt to taste

3 (15-ounce) cans cannellini or white navy beans, drained and rinsed

3 cloves garlic, minced

20 basil leaves

1. Preheat the oven to 350 degrees.

2. Arrange the tomatoes in a single layer on 4-quart temp-tations® dish. Pour the olive oil over and toss to thoroughly coat. Season with salt.

3. Bake until the tomatoes begin to shrink, about 45 minutes.

4. Gently add the beans to the tomatoes. Add the garlic and basil leaves, turning gently to combine.

TARA'S TIDBITS™ *If you'd like to make it a meal, add some cheese, such as crumbled feta; and you can always add whichever vegetables are in season, such as zucchini. A great take-along dish.*

SIDES

Curried Sweet Potato Fries

Easy to make, easy to multiply, and a real crowd-pleaser, these are a healthy alternative to standard fries—especially when I bake them using canola oil.

2 large sweet potatoes, peeled, ends trimmed

1 tablespoon canola oil

1 large egg white

2 teaspoons curry powder

½ teaspoon ground cumin

¼ teaspoon crushed red pepper flakes

1. Preheat to 400 degrees with rack in the center of the oven.

2. Place the sweet potato on a cutting board so that it is standing vertically on one of the trimmed ends. Cut the potato from top to bottom into ⅓-inch slices. Stack the slices, two at a time, and cut into ⅓-inch slices to make fries. Repeat with the remaining potato.

3. Place the potatoes in a large bowl and drizzle with oil; toss to coat. Set aside. In a medium bowl, whisk the egg white until frothy. Whisk in the curry powder, cumin, and red pepper flakes. Pour the egg white mixture over the fries and toss to coat.

4. Scatter the fries in a single layer on a temp-tations® Lid-it® and bake to desired crispness, about 50 minutes.

TARA'S TRADITIONS *It's that little hint of hot red pepper flakes that gives these comforting fries a kick. Never a leftover in my house!*

SIDES

Creamed Leeks

Mild, creamy, easy to prepare, and beautiful with the browned bread crumbs on top. Nutmeg gives this dish—a city cousin to that Thanksgiving-dinner staple, creamed onions—a subtly spiced flavor.

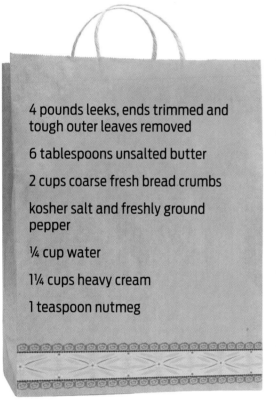

4 pounds leeks, ends trimmed and tough outer leaves removed

6 tablespoons unsalted butter

2 cups coarse fresh bread crumbs

kosher salt and freshly ground pepper

¼ cup water

1¼ cups heavy cream

1 teaspoon nutmeg

1. Preheat oven to 450 degrees with the rack positioned in the middle.

2. Trim the tops away from the leeks so that each is about 8 inches long. Halve lengthwise and cut crosswise into 1½-inch pieces. Fill a large bowl with cold water and plunge the leek pieces into it, swirling them around to release any trapped sand and dirt. Lift the leeks out of the water with a large slotted spoon. Repeat, then transfer leeks to a strainer and drain well.

3. In a large skillet over medium heat, melt 3 tablespoons butter. Add the bread crumbs and salt and pepper to taste. Cook, stirring often, until the bread crumbs are crisp and golden, 4 minutes. Set aside.

4. In a nonstick pan over medium-low heat, melt the remaining 3 tablespoons butter. Add the leeks and water, cover, and cook, stirring occasionally, until the leeks are tender, 10 to 12 minutes. Using a slotted spoon, transfer the leeks to a 4-quart temp-tations® dish and pour the cream slowly over them. Season with the nutmeg. Scatter the bread crumbs on top.

5. Bake until the cream is bubbling and slightly thickened and the bread crumbs are deep golden, about 15 minutes. Serve warm.

TARA'S TIDBITS™ *You can make this dish lighter by substituting light cream. I mix equal parts heavy cream and 2% milk to make 1¼ cups and whisk in 2 tablepoons flour so the texture is perfect.*

SIDES

Baked Acorn Squash with Maple Syrup and Walnuts

This has always been an autumn staple in our home. Maple syrup and walnuts make a wonderful combination, and the walnuts make it more of a meal.

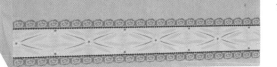

2 acorn squash, halved and seeds scraped away

½ cup maple syrup

2 tablespoons unsalted butter

2 tablespoons brown sugar

¼ teaspoon allspice

¼ golden raisins, optional

¼ cup walnut pieces

1. Preheat oven to 500 degrees.

2. Place the squash halves flesh side up in a 4-quart temp-tations® dish and roast until the flesh is fork-tender, about 1 hour.

3. Meanwhile, combine the maple syrup, butter, brown sugar, allspice, and golden raisins (if using) in a small saucepan and bring to a boil, stirring, until sugar is dissolved.

4. Brush the insides of the squash with the maple syrup mixture and return squash to oven; cook 5 minutes. Serve warm, topped with walnut pieces.

SIDES

TARA'S TIDBITS™ *Try adding 3 tablespoons currants to the maple syrup mixture in step 3.*

 **PREP TIME: 15 mins**

 **COOK TIME: 35 mins**

 SERVES: 6

 temp·tations
PRESENTABLE OVENWARE
by Tara

4 QUART

Mom's Brussels Sprouts with Bacon and Lemon

Unbelievably delicious! The colors of this dish are vibrant. Bacon, did anyone say bacon? Can you believe I really didn't like Brussels sprouts growing up until Mom made them? Now you know why!

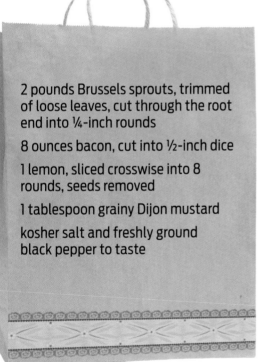

2 pounds Brussels sprouts, trimmed of loose leaves, cut through the root end into ¼-inch rounds

8 ounces bacon, cut into ½-inch dice

1 lemon, sliced crosswise into 8 rounds, seeds removed

1 tablespoon grainy Dijon mustard

kosher salt and freshly ground black pepper to taste

1. Preheat oven to 400 degrees.

2. Bring a 6-quart pot of salted water to a boil. Cook the Brussels sprouts until crisp-tender, 3 to 5 minutes. Transfer to a colander to drain.

3. Meanwhile, spread the bacon in a single layer in a 4-quart temp-tations® dish and bake until browned and not quite crispy, about 5 minutes. Add the Brussels sprouts and lemon slices and toss until thoroughly combined and the Brussels sprouts are coated in the bacon fat.

4. Roast until the Brussels sprouts begin to brown, stirring occasionally, about 20 minutes. Add the mustard and stir to thoroughly coat. Season with salt and pepper to taste. Serve warm.

TARA'S TIDBITS™ *A generous tablespoon of mustard, stirred in just before serving, gives these a subtle heat. If you want to keep this recipe on the lighter side, try using a poultry-based bacon or turkey bacon.*

SIDES

PREP TIME: 12 mins

COOK TIME: 35 mins

SERVES: 8

temp·tations.
PRESENTABLE OVENWARE
by Tara

1.5 QUART

Whipped Cauliflower

Smooth and creamy, this is a great low-carb alternative for mashed potatoes. I try to limit my carbs and have found this alternative to be even better than the real thing.

1 large head of cauliflower (about 2¾ pounds), cut into 1-inch florets

1 teaspoon kosher salt

½ cup heavy cream

1 fresh or dried bay leaf

1 teaspoon lemon zest

1 tablespoon minced fresh herbs (such as Italian parsley, thyme, chives)

2 tablespoons unsalted butter

¼ teaspoon freshly ground pepper

1. Preheat oven to 400 degrees.

2. In a large saucepan over medium-high heat, bring 1 cup of water, cauliflower, and ½ teaspoon of salt to a boil. Cover, reduce heat to medium, and cook, stirring once, until cauliflower is tender, about 10 minutes.

3. Remove cauliflower to a food processor or blender, discard liquid, and reserve pot. Scald cream: bring cream, bay leaf, lemon zest, and mixed herbs to a boil over medium high heat. Remove from heat, add butter, and let stand 5 minutes. Remove bay leaf.

4. Add cream mixture to cauliflower and pulse until smooth, about 1 minute. Adjust salt and pepper to taste. Transfer puree to temp-tations® 1.5-quart dish and bake until heated through, 10 to 12 minutes.

TARA'S TIDBITS™ *You can make this dish ahead and freeze it. This simple recipe has lots of options for add-ins: try parmesan or a teaspoon of lemon zest and 1 tablespoon of your favorite fresh herb medley. Also, you can lighten the calories by using the steaming liquid (about ¼ cup) and reducing cream to ¼ cup. Have fun with it!*

SIDES

Corn with Spiced Chili Pepper Mayonnaise

Who doesn't love street vendor food? This particular dish is called "elote" in Mexico, and it's a great family dish. The combination of pepper and chilies gives the corn a smoky, sweet, spicy kick, and I love anything with mayo!

4 ears of corn, shucked

¼ teaspoon kosher salt

⅔ cup mayonnaise

2 or 3 jarred roasted bell peppers (about 2 ounces)

1 tablespoon plus 1 teaspoon adobo sauce

1 lime, zested

¼ cup grated Cotija cheese (or another grating cheese, such as parmesan)

pinch sweet paprika

1. In a large 12-inch skillet over high heat, bring 1 cup of water to a boil with a pinch of salt. Add corn, cover, and reduce heat to medium-high. Steam until water is evaporated and corn is tender and bright yellow, 8 to 10 minutes.

2. Meanwhile, in a blender, combine mayonnaise, red bell peppers, adobo sauce, and lime zest. Process until smooth.

3. Remove corn to Lid-it® and skewer with temp-tations® corn skewers.

4. Spread mayo on corn to coat. Sprinkle with cheese and paprika and serve hot.

SIDES

TARA'S TIDBITS™ *Cotija cheese can be found in most grocery stores, but if you can't find it, no worries—use parmesan.*

Baked Scallop Stuffing

This recipe has been in my family for generations and is sometimes just a refreshing change from the usual holiday dressings. It's a family favorite that we make any time of the year.

3 tablespoons unsalted butter, plus more for pan

1 medium onion, cut into medium dice

1 red bell pepper, cut into medium dice

2 celery stalks, cut into medium dice

8 ounces day-old white bread, cut into ½–inch cubes (about 5 cups)

12 ounces fresh sea scallops, coarsely chopped

1 cup seafood stock

1 large egg, lightly beaten

1 tablespoon seafood seasoning, such as Old Bay®

1. Preheat oven to 375 degrees.

2. Lightly coat a 2.5-quart temp-tations® dish with butter and set aside.

3. In a large skillet over medium heat, melt the butter. Add the onion, red pepper, and celery. Cook, stirring occasionally, until vegetables begin to soften, about 5 minutes.

4. Transfer the vegetable mixture to a large bowl and let cool slightly, 5 minutes. Add the bread cubes, scallops, seafood stock, egg, and seafood seasoning, mixing to combine. Transfer stuffing to the prepared dish.

5. Bake until golden brown on top, 40 to 45 minutes.

TARA'S TRADITIONS *We also make this as a main meal, but it's equally lovely alongside your favorite fish and vegetables.*

SIDES

| PREP TIME: 15 mins | COOK TIME: 1 hour 20 mins | SERVES: 6 | 2.5 QUART |

Root Vegetable Bake-Up

Sooooo GOOD, sooooo EASY. I know it's just a bunch of root vegetables, but this is REALLY GOOD, and a nice change from the same old dishes we seem to make.

unsalted butter for the dish

12 ounces Yukon gold potatoes, peeled and sliced into ⅛-inch-thick rounds

1 medium parsnip, peeled and sliced into ⅛-inch-thick rounds

2 medium carrots, peeled and sliced into ⅛-inch-thick rounds

12 ounces sweet potatoes, peeled and sliced into ⅛-inch-thick rounds

6 ounces Swiss cheese, grated (2 cups)

1 teaspoon dried thyme leaves

kosher salt and freshly ground black pepper to taste

½ cup heavy cream

½ cup low-sodium chicken stock

1. Preheat oven to 375 degrees. Lightly coat a 2.5-quart temp-tations® dish with butter and set aside.

2. Layer the vegetables into the prepared dish, sprinkling each layer with cheese, thyme, salt, and pepper.

3. Pour the cream and chicken stock into the dish and cover with foil.

4. Bake, covered, 1 hour. Remove the foil and bake until the vegetables are tender and the cheese is bubbly, 15 to 20 minutes.

5. Let cool slightly before serving.

TARA'S TIDBITS™ *This recipe has really good color; it's healthy and can be adapted to any veggies on hand. It's a great compliment to any beef main course such as a rib roast. The smaller you cut the vegetables, the shorter the cooking time, so a medium dice will shorten to 45–50 minutes.*

SIDES

PREP TIME: 10 mins

COOK TIME: 40 mins

SERVES: 6

temp·tations
PRESENTABLE OVENWARE
by Tara
4 QUART

Mom's Roasted Cauliflower with Pine Nuts and Parsley

Whether it's the roasting, or the combination of the pine nuts—or the combination of the two—this is a memorable dish, which is saying a lot, since, after all, this is just cauliflower. Outstanding!

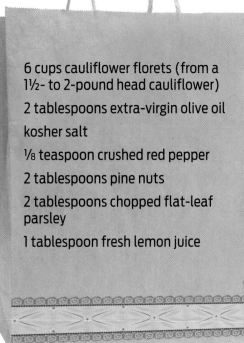

6 cups cauliflower florets (from a 1½- to 2-pound head cauliflower)

2 tablespoons extra-virgin olive oil

kosher salt

⅛ teaspoon crushed red pepper

2 tablespoons pine nuts

2 tablespoons chopped flat-leaf parsley

1 tablespoon fresh lemon juice

1. Preheat oven to 375 degrees.

2. Place the cauliflower into a 4-quart temp-tations® dish. Add the olive oil, ½ teaspoon salt, and the red pepper, tossing to coat. Bake, tossing once halfway through, until golden brown, 30 to 40 minutes.

3. Meanwhile, in a small skillet, over medium-low heat, toast the pine nuts, stirring constantly until light golden brown, about 4 minutes. Transfer to a small bowl and set aside.

4. Top the roasted cauliflower with the pine nuts and chopped parsley, and drizzle with lemon juice. Serve warm or at room temperature.

TARA'S TRADITIONS *This is one of my favorite side dishes, especially on a chilly night, accompanied by Brussels sprouts and roasted chicken. It's always important to me that food on the plate works well together colorwise.*

Keep your eye on the pine nuts; they can be easy to burn. Once you smell them it's probably too late!

SIDES

Onion Ring Bake

This is a great and easy side dish with fewer calories than the deep-fried version. It's AMAZING, crispy on the outside and tender on the inside. Let's face it, we all deserve a treat!

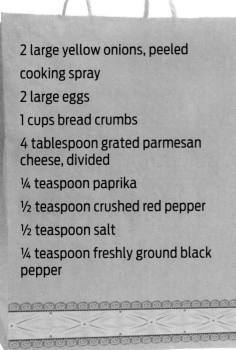

2 large yellow onions, peeled

cooking spray

2 large eggs

1 cups bread crumbs

4 tablespoon grated parmesan cheese, divided

¼ teaspoon paprika

½ teaspoon crushed red pepper

½ teaspoon salt

¼ teaspoon freshly ground black pepper

1. Preheat the oven to 450 degrees.

2. Cut onions into ½-inch circles; separate into rings and place in a large bowl. Cover and chill in the refrigerator 30 minutes.

3. Spray a 4-quart temp-tations® dish lightly with cooking spray; set aside. In a small mixing bowl, beat the eggs.

4. In another shallow bowl, combine bread crumbs with 3 tablespoons parmesan, paprika, red pepper flakes, salt, and pepper. Dip each of the onions, one at a time, into the egg, letting the excess drip off, and then dip into the bread crumb mixture, turning to coat. Transfer onions to prepared dish.

5. Spray canola oil evenly over rings and bake until golden brown, 20 minutes. Immediately sprinkle with remaining parmesan cheese on top.

TARA'S TRADITIONS *Mom came up with this recipe (thanks, Mom!) and likes to serve them standing up in individual small bowls.*

For a quick dipping sauce, combine equal parts ketchup and mayo; serve with warm onion rings.

SIDES

Taco Rolls

These are great when you have unexpected guests because most of the ingredients are already in your pantry. Improvise if you're missing one or two ingredients and have a fiesta! Growing up, we always had a "taco" night, which I loved. This brings me back to being a kid again—and did I mention it's yummy?

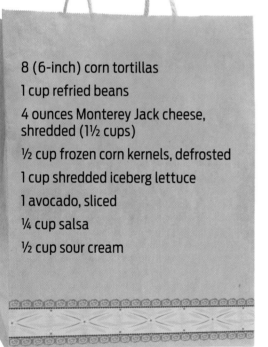

8 (6-inch) corn tortillas

1 cup refried beans

4 ounces Monterey Jack cheese, shredded (1½ cups)

½ cup frozen corn kernels, defrosted

1 cup shredded iceberg lettuce

1 avocado, sliced

¼ cup salsa

½ cup sour cream

1. Preheat oven to 375 degrees.

2. Wrap a few of the tortillas between two paper towels and microwave on high until pliable, about 30 seconds.

3. Spread 2 tablespoons refried beans onto a tortilla. Top with 1 tablespoon cheese and 1 tablespoon corn. Roll the tortilla up and place, seam side down, in a 4-quart temp-tations® dish. Repeat with the remaining tortillas, beans, cheese, and corn. Top with the remaining cheese.

4. Bake until the tortillas are beginning to crisp at the edges and the cheese is melted, 20 minutes.

5. Remove from the oven and top with lettuce, avocado, salsa, and sour cream.

TARA'S TIDBITS™ *I serve these frequently as an appetizer or as a side with a bowl of chili.*

SIDES

Desserts

Red Eye Brownie Pudding Pie

It's the simple things; so simple, but so good. This one will definitely cure your chocolate craving, and I've added a secret ingredient that makes this pudding pie unique, moist, and tasty.

nonstick cooking spray

1 cup all-purpose flour

½ teaspoon salt

4 ounces unsweetened chocolate

2 tablespoons instant espresso powder

2 sticks (8 ounces) unsalted butter

4 large eggs, lightly beaten

1 cup packed dark brown sugar

1 cup granulated sugar

1 tablespoon vanilla extract

¾ cup walnuts

powdered sugar, for dusting

1. Preheat oven to 350 degrees. Spray a 9-inch temp-tations® pie plate with nonstick cooking spray. In a medium bowl whisk the flour and salt together; set aside.

2. In a separate medium bowl placed over a medium pot filled with 1 inch of gently simmering water, melt the chocolate, espresso powder, and the butter together, stirring to combine. Meanwhile, in a separate large bowl whisk the lightly beaten eggs with both sugars and the vanilla; set aside. Whisk the chocolate mixture into the egg mixture.

3. Using a rubber spatula, gently fold the flour mixture and walnuts into the chocolate mixture. Do not overmix.

4. Pour batter into the prepared dish and bake until a toothpick inserted near the edge of the pie (not the middle, which should remain a bit pudding-like) comes out with moist crumbs, 50 to 60 minutes. Cool for 20 minutes and dust with powdered sugar. Serve warm with vanilla ice cream.

TARA'S TIDBITS™ *This is a great recipe for spur-of-the-moment dinner guests—but then again, how many of your guests don't like most things chocolate?*

For extra-tasty Brownie Pudding Pie, toast the walnuts in a 350-degree oven on a cookie sheet until fragrant, about 10 minutes.

DESSERTS

Old World Fashioned Apple Crisp

This recipe means the world to me. Besides being decadently delicious, it was developed in the very first pattern, Old World, of temp-tations® presentable ovenware™!

nonstick cooking spray

5 large apples (about 9 cups) peeled, cored, and cut into ¼- to ½-inch wedges

¼ cup water

¼ cup bottled lemon juice, well shaken

½ cup packed dark brown sugar

2 teaspoons cinnamon

1 teaspoon salt

1½ cups all-purpose flour

1½ cups granulated sugar

2 sticks unsalted butter, softened

1. Preheat oven to 375 degrees and spray a temp-tations® 3-quart dish with nonstick cooking spray.

2. In prepared pan, toss apples with water, lemon juice, dark brown sugar, cinnamon, and salt.

3. Make the topping: in a separate bowl, combine flour, granulated sugar, and butter. Use your fingers to form small, crumbly clumps of topping. Cover apples with topping and bake until crisp is browned and bubbling, 60 to 70 minutes.

4. Let cool at least 15 minutes before serving.

TARA'S TRADITIONS *It means a lot to me to share this special recipe that has brought our family and friends so much joy and love. Use your favorite apples, such as Granny Smith or, in the fall, Cortland or Macoun.*

DESSERTS

*This is a photo of me when I was in ninth grade with crazy hair!
I thought I was the bomb. I was definitely a child of the '80s. My
father used to say, "You use so much hairspray, that if you went
out in a windstorm you would snap your neck off!"*

PREP TIME: 15 mins

COOK TIME: 15 mins

SERVES: 6

temp·tations
PRESENTABLE OVENWARE
by Tara
SIX 6-OZ. DISHES

Perfect Butterscotch Pudding

Dessert time is a sacred time in my house. I absolutely adore butterscotch pudding; it reminds me of my childhood! This butterscotch pudding perfectly captures that brown sugar–butter combo that's so nostalgic and intensely satisfying. While the recipe makes six servings, you'll be hard pressed not to eat them all yourself. This was one of my dad's favorites.

1½ cups packed dark brown sugar

6 tablespoons cornstarch

2 teaspoons salt

2 cups heavy cream

2½ cups milk

2 large eggs

2 large egg yolks

6 tablespoons unsalted butter, softened

2 tablespoons plus 2 teaspoons vanilla

store-bought, slightly sweetened whipped cream

1. In a medium saucepot, whisk together dark brown sugar, cornstarch, and salt. Whisk in the heavy cream, milk, eggs, and yolks.

2. Cook over medium-high heat, whisking constantly, until mixture comes to a boil and begins to thicken, 5 to 10 minutes. Once mixture is boiling, whisk constantly for 1 to 2 minutes.

3. Remove pot from heat and whisk in butter and vanilla.

4. Pour pudding into six 6-ounce temp-tations® dishes. Cover individual puddings with plastic wrap to prevent a skin from forming. Chill in refrigerator until firm and cold, 2 hours. Serve with whipped cream.

TARA'S TIDBITS™ *This recipe is easy, affordable, and utilizes very common ingredients. It's one of those delightful little recipes that requires no effort, but makes you a dessert temp-tationista in the eyes of those you serve it to.*

The extra salt and vanilla in this recipe makes for a super butterscotchy flavored pudding.

DESSERTS

PREP TIME: 20 mins   **COOK TIME: 20 mins**   **SERVES: 12**   **MUFFIN PAN**

Brodie's Stuffed Devil's Food Cupcakes

This one is a family classic. The rich chocolate pairs perfectly with the sweet cream cheese filling. These cupcakes are phenomenal!

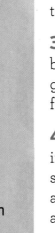

CUPCAKE INGREDIENTS
1 cup packed dark brown sugar
1 cup flour
⅓ cup cocoa powder, sifted
1 teaspoon baking powder
½ teaspoon baking soda
½ teaspoon salt
½ cup boiling water
1½ teaspoon espresso powder
1 egg
1 teaspoon vanilla
½ cup buttermilk
¼ cup vegetable oil

FILLING INGREDIENTS
1 (8-ounce) package regular cream cheese
1 egg
¼ cup granulated sugar

1. Preheat oven to 350 degrees and line the muffin pan with paper cupcake liners. In a medium bowl, whisk together dark brown sugar, flour, sifted cocoa powder, baking powder, baking soda, and salt. Set aside.

2. In a large bowl, add espresso powder to boiling water and stir to combine. Add the egg, vanilla, buttermilk, and oil and whisk until thoroughly combined.

3. Add the flour and sugar mixture to the egg and buttermilk mixture and, with a rubber spatula, fold gently to combine. Fill the muffin cups ⅔ of the way full and set aside.

4. For the filling, beat together all of the filling ingredients on medium speed with a hand mixer or a stand mixer fitted with the paddle attachment, until almost smooth, scraping down the mixing bowl with a rubber spatula as needed.

5. Put a rounded tablespoon of filling in the center of each filled cup. Bake for 18 to 20 minutes, or until a toothpick inserted in the side of the cupcake comes out clean. Let cool to room temperature before serving.

TARA'S TRADITIONS *Family includes my godson Brodie and you can tell from this photo this is one of Brodie's favorites! This recipe serves 12 but by the time my favorite little devil is finished "helping," Auntie Tara is lucky to have one!*

When testing the cupcakes for doneness, insert a toothpick in the side of the cupcake, not in the cream cheese center, as the center remains quite moist.

DESSERTS

This is my godson Brodie

He loves to help his auntie Tara bake his favorite devil's food cupcakes.

Obviously, the best part of making these cupcakes is when I hand Brodie the bowl (of course I add the raw egg after and always wait until his parents leave the room) because my little helper KNOWS that eating the batter out of the bowl is the most important part of the entire helping process.

It takes only 20 minutes to prepare these cupcakes and about 20 minutes to bake them but that isn't nearly enough time for my Brodie to get all of the batter out of his bowl and off of his cute little face!

And then comes the fun part—decorating his cupcakes with that special flower I designed for the Old World pattern back in 2003.

Although Brodie is just a baby, he's really smart and loves to count out all of the yellow and red M&M's® that go on top of all dozen cupcakes. We make these so many times that Brodie remembers that we need sixty yellow and twelve red ones! He's so proud that he thought of filling his cupcakes all by himself with his special ingredient, cream cheese!

This photo of (left to right: Mom, Bimbi, Grandma Maria)
was taken at Christmas, Grandma Maria's favorite holiday.
(I think her sweater might be a clue ☺) I've included a
lot of their favorite recipes in this cookbook, including
Bimbi bars because they're family favorites. When I make
them, the aroma that fills my home brings back memories
and everything seems to get just a little bit brighter!

Bimbi Bars

My second mother Bimbi's house was always open to every kid on the block. She always made sure to have her pantry stocked with ingredients so she could teach us to make something we not only all loved, but weren't allowed to eat at home until after dinner!

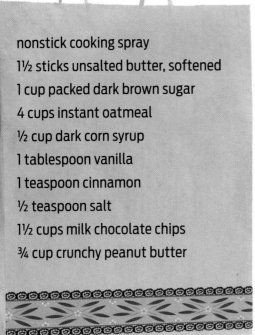

nonstick cooking spray

1½ sticks unsalted butter, softened

1 cup packed dark brown sugar

4 cups instant oatmeal

½ cup dark corn syrup

1 tablespoon vanilla

1 teaspoon cinnamon

½ teaspoon salt

1½ cups milk chocolate chips

¾ cup crunchy peanut butter

1. Preheat oven to 350 degrees and spray a temptations® 4-quart dish with nonstick cooking spray. In a large bowl, using a hand mixer on medium speed or a stand mixer fitted with a paddle attachment, cream the butter and sugar together until fully incorporated, scraping down the sides of the bowl as needed.

2. Add the oatmeal, corn syrup, vanilla, cinnamon, and salt; beat until combined.

3. Transfer dough to prepared dish and, using your fingers, press into bottom of dish. Bake until bars begin to brown and are starting to set, 20 to 25 minutes. Remove and set aside.

4. While bars are setting, in a small pan over low heat (or in the microwave on high), melt the chocolate and peanut butter, stirring often (about every 20 seconds) to prevent burning.

5. Pour melted topping over warm bars, spreading evenly. Refrigerate until firm, about two hours. Slice into squares and serve.

TARA'S TRADITIONS *These Bimbi Bars are some of my fondest childhood memories. I absolutely loved them and always keep my house open to every kid on the block and my pantry stocked so that I, too, can teach them to make what they're not allowed to eat at home until after dinner!*

When spreading the chocolate peanut butter topping on the warm base, do so gently, as the base will be quite soft. The base firms up beautifully after refrigeration.

DESSERTS

Banana Splits Bars

For a taste reminiscent of those Friday night drive-thrus, these delicious bars will be quickly added to your list of favorites. They're extremely easy to make so you might want to double up on this one!

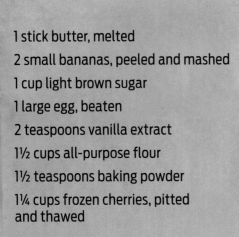

1 stick butter, melted

2 small bananas, peeled and mashed

1 cup light brown sugar

1 large egg, beaten

2 teaspoons vanilla extract

1½ cups all-purpose flour

1½ teaspoons baking powder

1¼ cups frozen cherries, pitted and thawed

1. Preheat oven 350 degrees.

2. In an electric blender, mix the butter, banana, brown sugar, egg, and vanilla extract.

3. Add flour and baking powder to the mixture and beat for about 1 minute. Gently fold in the cherries.

4. Pour batter into the ovenware and bake for 40–45 minutes, or until a toothpick inserted into the center comes out clean. Let cool before cutting into 9 equal squares.

TARA'S TIDBITS™ *I love to drizzle any store-bought chocolate syrup on top of these delish bars and when I really want to be decadent, I add a dollop of whipped cream!*

DESSERTS

Blueberry Cornmeal Crumble

Quick and easy—I love this blueberry crumble not only because it feeds a crowd but because it can be served any time of the year and any time of the day!

4 tablespoons unsalted butter, plus more for the dish

16 ounces frozen blueberries

3 tablespoons cornstarch

¼ cup granulated sugar

2 tablespoons fresh lemon juice

1¼ cups Jiffy® cornbread mix from 1 (8½-ounce) box

¼ cup packed light brown sugar

½ cup heavy cream

1. Preheat oven to 375 degrees. Lightly coat six 6-ounce dipping dishes with butter, place on a baking sheet, and set aside.

2. In a medium-sized bowl, combine the blueberries, cornstarch, granulated sugar, and lemon juice. Toss to combine and thoroughly coat berries. Divide the blueberry mixture into the prepared dipping dishes.

3. In a separate medium-sized bowl, combine the cornbread mix, brown sugar, and butter. Use your hands to work the butter into the dry ingredients until large crumbles form. Sprinkle the crumble mixture over the blueberries.

4. Bake 35 to 40 minutes, or until the crumble topping is golden brown and the berry juices are bubbling.

5. Meanwhile, in the bowl of a stand mixer fitted with the whisk attachment, beat the cream on medium-high speed until soft peaks form, about 2 minutes. Serve with whipped cream.

TARA'S TRADITIONS *Blueberries are quite possibly one of the healthiest foods around so it's a great one to serve to the kids. I'll sometimes substitute frozen yogurt instead of the whipped cream for one of my backwards banquet recipes!*

DESSERTS

John David and Alexandra Maria are my nephew
and niece and love to bake just like their auntie.
You can't keep either one of them out of the kitchen;
I think it's in the genes. Just look at their smiles.

PREP TIME: 15 mins **COOK TIME: 20 to 25 mins** **SERVES: 20 to 24** **2.5 QUART**

Mademoiselle Alexandra Maria's Magic Ginger Sparkle Bars

These bars are just like my niece Alexandra Maria, plenty sweet and just the right amount of spirit. These are really moist, gingery, and more like a cake than a bar.

BAR INGREDIENTS
nonstick cooking spray

¾ cup vegetable shortening

1 cup packed dark brown sugar

1 egg yolk

¼ cup molasses

2 cups flour

1 tablespoon ginger

1 teaspoon cinnamon

⅛ teaspoon cayenne (secret ingredient!)

½ teaspoon salt

2 teaspoons baking soda

GLAZE INGREDIENTS
2 cups powdered sugar

3 tablespoons milk

1. Preheat oven to 350 degrees and spray a 2.5-quart temp-tations® dish with nonstick cooking spray. On medium speed, cream the shortening and sugar together with a hand mixer or a stand mixer fitted with the paddle attachment, until fluffy; scraping down the mixing bowl with a rubber spatula as needed.

2. Add the yolk and molasses and beat until fully incorporated, scraping down the mixing bowl with a rubber spatula as needed.

3. In a separate bowl, whisk together the flour, ginger, cinnamon, cayenne, salt, and baking soda and, with the mixer on low speed, slowly add this dry mixture to the mixing bowl, beating just until incorporated.

4. Transfer to the prepared pan and, using your fingers, press dough into the bottom of the pan. Bake for 20 to 25 minutes, or until a toothpick inserted into the center comes out with moist crumbs.

5. To make the glaze: Whisk together the powdered sugar and milk. Pour glaze over the warm bars and let them come to room temperature before slicing and serving.

DESSERTS

TARA'S TIDBITS™ *These bars are so moist and flavorful. They are so easy to make and delicious! Not only are they delicious, your house will smell wonderful too!*

Baking for 20 to 25 minutes produces a chewy bar; if you prefer a crispier bar, bake for 25 to 30 minutes.

Easy Lemon Sheet Cake

This is a really delicious, super-moist cake with a lot of lemon flavor. Mom and I often take it to get-togethers, and because there's never any left, I wanted to be sure to include this favorite of ours in this cookbook.

CAKE INGREDIENTS

nonstick cooking spray

1½ cups cake flour

5 tablespoons unsalted butter, softened

1¾ cups sugar

7 tablespoons vegetable oil

2 eggs

3 egg yolks

1 teaspoon vanilla

¼ cup bottled lemon juice, well shaken

1 cup lemon yogurt

1 cup flour

2 teaspoons baking powder

½ teaspoon salt

GLAZE INGREDIENTS

3 cups powdered sugar

⅓ cup bottled lemon juice, well shaken

1. Preheat oven to 325 degrees and spray a 4-quart temp-tations® dish with nonstick cooking spray. Dust the pan with flour, knocking out any excess. On medium speed, cream the butter, sugar, and oil together until light and fluffy, about 5 minutes; scraping down the mixing bowl with a rubber spatula as needed.

2. Add the eggs and yolks one at a time, waiting until each addition is fully incorporated and scraping down the mixing bowl with a rubber spatula as needed. Add the vanilla and beat until combined.

3. In a small bowl, whisk the lemon juice and yogurt together and set aside. In a separate bowl, sift the flour, cake flour, baking powder, and salt together and, on low speed, add the flour mixture to the mixing bowl in three additions, alternating with the lemon juice/yogurt mixture, and beginning and ending with the flour mixture. Scrape down the mixing bowl with a rubber spatula as needed. Beat on medium speed for a few seconds more, until batter is smooth.

4. Transfer the batter to the prepared dish and bake for 50 to 55 minutes or until a toothpick inserted in the center comes out clean.

5. To make the glaze: Whisk the powdered sugar and lemon juice together. Using a toothpick, poke holes in the warm cake and coat with glaze. Let the cake come to room temperature before slicing with a sharp paring knife and serving.

TARA'S TIDBITS™ *The frosting on this one is my favorite part! It's also great to make for kids and fun to have them help you decorate it with their favorite toppings, such as colored sprinkles, coconut, white chocolate chips....*

DESSERTS

Pecan Chocolate Pie Bars

I'm from upstate New York and have been told by our southern friends that these bars are exactly what pecan bars should be. They asked ME for the recipe. Pecan pie is always a favorite with my family, and since I am a big fan of portions, I love these individual bars.

nonstick cooking spray

1½ sticks unsalted butter, softened, plus 2 tablespoons, melted separately

2 cups all-purpose flour

½ cup packed light brown sugar

½ teaspoon salt

2 large eggs

1 egg yolk

¾ cup light corn syrup

¼ cup granulated sugar

¼ cup packed dark brown sugar

1 package semi-sweet chocolate chips

2 cups chopped pecans

¼ teaspoon orange zest (from half of 1 orange)

1. Preheat oven to 350 degrees and spray a temptations® 3.5-quart dish with nonstick spray. Line the bottom and ends of the dish with parchment paper and spray again.

2. With a hand mixer on medium speed or a stand mixer fitted with the paddle attachment, cream the 1½ sticks of butter, flour, light brown sugar, and salt until incorporated, scraping down the sides of the bowl as needed. Transfer mixture to the prepared dish and press firmly into bottom of dish.

3. Bake until firm to the touch and lightly browned, 30 to 35 minutes. Let cool 10 minutes. Meanwhile, in a separate bowl, whisk together melted butter, eggs, yolk, corn syrup, granulated sugar, dark brown sugar, chocolate chips, pecans, and orange zest until combined.

4. Pour topping onto slightly cooled crust and bake until set and bubbling all over, 40 to 45 minutes.

5. Let cool to room temperature before slicing and serving.

TARA'S TIDBITS™ *Everyone loves these pecan bars, especially with the delicious combination of pecans and chocolate.*

For extra-tasty Chocolate Pecan Pie Bars, toast the pecans in a 350-degree oven, on a cookie sheet, until fragrant, about 10 minutes.

DESSERTS

PREP TIME: 20 mins   **COOK TIME: 80 mins**   **SERVES: 16**   **LOAF PAN**

Raspberry Swirl Pound Cake

Hello delicious…you had me at raspberry. The swirls of raspberry and pound cake are an awesome pairing. This is a seriously delicious pound cake, and I love how pretty each piece looks when it's cut and plated.

nonstick cooking spray

1½ cups plus 2 tablespoons all-purpose flour, divided

1¼ sticks unsalted butter, softened

1 cup plus 2 tablespoons sugar and 3 tablespoons sugar, divided

2 eggs

1 egg yolk

1½ teaspoons vanilla extract

½ teaspoon baking powder

½ teaspoon salt

⅔ cup heavy cream

1½ cups frozen raspberries, defrosted

1. Preheat oven to 350 degrees and spray a temptations® loaf pan with nonstick cooking spray. Line the bottom and ends of the pan with parchment paper, allowing the paper to extend over the edge of the pan, spray again. Dust the pan with 2 tablespoons of flour, knocking out any excess.

2. In a large bowl, with a mixer on high speed, cream the butter and 1 cup plus 2 tablespoons sugar together until fluffy, about 5 minutes, scraping down mixing bowl as needed. Reduce to medium speed; beat in the eggs and yolk, one at a time, beating for one minute after each addition. Scrape down the mixing bowl and add the vanilla; beat until fully incorporated.

3. In a separate bowl, whisk together the 1½ cups flour, baking powder, and salt. On low speed, add the dry ingredients to the bowl in three additions, alternating with the heavy cream, and beginning and ending with the dry ingredients. Scrape down the bowl as needed. Combine the raspberries and 3 tablespoons of sugar in a food processor and puree.

4. Transfer a little over half of the batter to the prepared pan and smooth the top. Spoon half the raspberry puree over the batter in the pan. Add the other half of the batter, smooth, and spoon the rest of the puree on top. With a wooden skewer or a thin knife, swirl the puree. Be sure your skewer extends into the second layer of puree, too.

5. Bake until set or until a toothpick inserted in the center comes out clean, 75 to 80 minutes. Once the cake has cooled completely, lift out of pan with the parchment paper, and serve.

TARA'S TIDBITS™ *If they're in season and readily available, substitute fresh raspberries for the frozen.*

DESSERTS

Zucchini Cake with Chocolate Chips

I cannot stop eating this cake. I love a heavier, moist cake and this one definitely falls into that category. No one ever guesses there is zucchini in this cake! It disappears into a warm, moist, delicious desert; amazing!

nonstick cooking spray

1 cup packed dark brown sugar

1 cup granulated sugar

1¼ cups vegetable oil

2 large eggs

2 large yolks

2 teaspoons vanilla extract

1¼ cups all-purpose flour

1½ teaspoons baking soda

2 teaspoons baking powder

2 teaspoons cinnamon

1 teaspoon salt

3 cups lightly packed grated zucchini (1 to 2 zucchini)

1 cup mini chocolate chips

powdered sugar, for dusting

1. Preheat oven to 350 degrees. Spray a temp-tations® 4-quart dish with nonstick cooking spray.

2. In a large bowl, whisk together the dark brown sugar, granulated sugar, and the oil until combined. Add the eggs, yolks, and vanilla; whisk until combined.

3. In a separate bowl, whisk together the flour, baking soda, baking powder, cinnamon, and salt. Add the grated zucchini and mini chocolate chips, stirring until chips and zucchini are coated in flour.

4. With a rubber spatula, fold the flour mixture into the egg mixture until just combined. Do not overmix.

5. Fill the prepared temp-tations® dish and bake until set, or until a toothpick inserted in the center comes out clean, 65 to 70 minutes. Cool cake completely, about 1 hour. Dust with powdered sugar and serve, sliced.

TARA'S TRADITIONS *Kids love this cake. When I know my godchildren will be visiting, mean Auntie Tara sneaks in blueberries and occasionally walnuts. It's a great way for them to get the benefits of vegetable, berries, and nuts in this delicious cake without them even suspecting it.*

Mini chips are used in this recipe because larger chips, or chunks, tend to sink to the bottom of the cake. To prevent even the mini chips from sinking, lightly spray them with nonstick cooking spray before tossing them in the flour—this adheres the flour to the chips and further prevents sinking.

DESSERTS

PREP TIME: 30 mins

COOK TIME: none

SERVES: 6

temp-tations
PRESENTABLE OVENWARE
by Tara
DIPPING DISHES

Macaylan's Fluffy Nutter "Wednesdae"

This sticky and gooey family-favorite treat is not only a walk down memory lane but a special bond between my goddaughter Macaylan and me. Since I don't have to be at the studio until evenings on Wednesdays, afternoons are always our special time together. One day Macaylan noticed a jar of Fluff® in my cabinet and asked if she could have a taste. I handed her a spoonful and she loved it! Before I send her home we always make what we call a "Wednesdae" (our secret version of a sundae), and we love this one the best! Of course when her mother caught Macaylan on her kitchen counter eating Fluff® out of the jar with a spoon she knew exactly where she'd learned that habit—Auntie Tara.

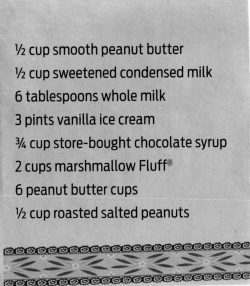

½ cup smooth peanut butter

½ cup sweetened condensed milk

6 tablespoons whole milk

3 pints vanilla ice cream

¾ cup store-bought chocolate syrup

2 cups marshmallow Fluff®

6 peanut butter cups

½ cup roasted salted peanuts

1. In a small saucepan, combine the peanut butter, condensed milk and milk and stir constantly over low heat until warmed through and smooth, about 6 to 8 minutes.

2. Pour two tablespoons of this sauce into the bottoms of 6 temp-tations® round dipping dishes. Scoop two large scoops of vanilla ice cream on top and place in the freezer 15 minutes or until cold and set.

3. Place the remaining peanut butter sauce, chocolate syrup, and marshmallow Fluff® in three separate large resealable plastic bags. Snip a small hole in the corner of the bag with the peanut butter sauce and a small hole in the bag with the chocolate syrup. Snip a large hole in the bag with the marshmallow Fluff®.

4. Remove the ice cream from the freezer and drizzle with the peanut butter sauce and chocolate syrup. Sprinkle with peanuts. Pipe some of the Fluff® on top and push a peanut butter cup into the Fluff®. Serve immediately.

TARA'S TRADITIONS *It doesn't get much better than this. We added sliced bananas to one Wednesdae and we loved that too. Feel free to make this Wednesdae your own, and know that it's not against the law to eat it on a Tuesdae, or a Sundae, etc.*

DESSERTS

Before I introduced Fluff®

to my deprived little godchild Macaylan, she was only allowed just plain peanut butter sandwiches.

After sharing our many special "Wednesdaes" together I decided to bring a jar of Fluff® to her house and introduce her to her very first peanut butter and Fluff® sandwich. She was hooked. From that day forward—can you blame her?—Macaylan never ate a plain peanut butter sandwich again. One afternoon Jenn was sitting in her living room when Macaylan came skipping in eating a big spoonful of Fluff®. Jenn was speechless and wondered where she possibly could have learned this trick...so she asked her. Innocently, Macaylan admitted that it was...I'll give you one guess! Of course...it was her auntie Tara!

It wasn't easy to explain to Macaylan that eating Fluff® on a spoon is a treat and not a snack. To this day Jenn laughs when Macaylan asks for her special "Auntie Tara" treat on a spoon! ☺

DESSERTS

Our Family's Famous Peach-Almond Cobbler

I'm a sucker for the classics. If you live in the South and manage to go an entire summer without eating a gallon of this, then you obviously have my sympathy. Peach cobbler is considered a southern classic. But almond has this way of captivating my taste buds. My entire family is addicted to this one.

3 (10-ounce) bags frozen peaches, thawed (about 6 cups)

¾ cup sugar

½ teaspoon pure almond extract

2 tablespoons cornstarch

1 cup all-purpose flour

1 teaspoon baking powder

½ teaspoon kosher salt

6 tablespoons cold unsalted butter, cut into small pieces

¼ cup whole milk

¼ cup sliced almonds

1. Preheat oven to 425 degrees. Place the peaches, ¼ cup sugar, almond extract, and cornstarch into a 2.5-quart temp-tations® dish, and toss to coat. Bake 10 minutes.

2. Meanwhile, in a medium bowl, whisk together the flour, ½ cup sugar, baking powder, and salt. Use your hands to work the butter into the dry ingredients until coarse crumbs form.

3. Stir the milk into the dry ingredients and mix until just combined.

4. Remove peaches from the oven. Drop spoonfuls of the batter over them and sprinkle with almonds.

5. Bake about 25 minutes, until the top is golden. Serve immediately.

TARA'S TRADITIONS *When you're looking for a really good "old-fashioned" recipe, I just know your family and guests will scream with delight, especially when it's topped off with whipped cream or vanilla ice cream.*

DESSERTS

Deana's Red Velvet Cupcakes

These are little versions of the classic red velvet cake. WOW! My guests really love when I bring these over, and they always tell me how moist they are. My friend Deana actually calls them criminal and is usually good for at least four. Glad she shared this recipe with me!

1⅓ cups all-purpose flour

1 teaspoon cocoa powder

½ teaspoon baking soda

½ teaspoon baking powder

1 cup sugar

⅓ cup vegetable oil

1 large egg

1 teaspoon red food coloring

1 cup buttermilk, well shaken

FROSTING

8 ounces cream cheese, at room temperature

2 ounces (½ stick) salted butter, at room temperature

2 cups powdered sugar

1. Preheat the oven to 350 degrees.

2. Sift all the dry ingredients into a large mixing bowl and make a well in the center.

3. In a separate medium bowl, whisk together the vegetable oil, egg, food coloring, and buttermilk until combined. Add the buttermilk mixture to the flour mixture, stirring just until smooth. Do not overmix.

4. Fill a temp-tations® 6-cup muffin dish halfway full and bake until set, or a toothpick inserted in the center comes out clean, 20 minutes. Remove cupcakes to a cooling rack and bake remaining cupcakes, repeating with remaining mixture.

5. Make the frosting: In a large bowl, with a hand mixer or in a stand mixer with the paddle attachment, on medium speed, beat the cream cheese, butter, and sugar, until light and fluffy. Spread or pipe onto cooled cupcakes.

by Luna

TARA'S TIDBITS™ *Don't have time to make cream cheese frosting? These moist cupcakes are delicious with just a delicate dusting of powdered sugar over the top—and you still get that dramatic red and white effect!*

DESSERTS

Trifecta Chocolate Chip Coconut Bars

An all-time favorite, with an interesting cocoa layer that gives a twist to this bar. You can also substitute any salted nut if you prefer a more savory treat. I've never met anyone who didn't love them. Even people who don't like coconut seem to love these! You can freeze them and they're awesome to eat even while frozen. In fact, I prefer them that way!

1 cup chopped walnuts

1½ cups graham cracker crumbs (9 crackers)

2 tablespoons cocoa powder

2 tablespoons cups sugar

1 tablespoon unsalted butter, melted

1 cup chocolate chips

½ cup white chocolate chips

½ cup butterscotch chips

1⅓ cups shredded coconut

1 (14-ounce) can condensed milk

1. Preheat oven to 350 degrees and place a rack in the center.

2. Toast walnuts in a temp-tations® dish until golden and aromatic for about 7 minutes.

3. Remove walnuts and butter the dish.

4. Mix together graham cracker crumbs, cocoa powder, and sugar in a bowl. Add melted butter to the graham cracker mixture and mix until crumbs are moist. Press the crumbs evenly onto the bottom of the dish.

5. Sprinkle walnuts, chocolate chips, white chocolate chips, butterscotch chips, and coconut over the graham crumbs.

6. Pour the condensed milk evenly over the entire mixture.

7. Bake for 25 minutes until golden brown.

8. Let to cool in the pan and cut into 15 (2½- by 3-inch) bars.

TARA'S TRADITIONS *This definitely is an old-fashioned favorite, one of those fast and easy standbys! I remember my mom making them and my grandmother before that. It's not like there are any complicated directions or measuring here. It's straightforward, and all the ingredients come together and complement each other.*

DESSERTS

Beautiful Gracie is my BFF Amy's daughter and my goddaughter. We love experimenting in the kitchen. I don't see nearly enough of her or her brother Joey, but when we do it's always unforgettable. It's probably best we don't live next door because they would be two very spoiled children.

DESSERTS

Gracie's Ginger Molasses Bread

Last Christmas my friend Amy and her daughter Gracie (my god-daughter) completely caught me off guard with a surprise visit to my home. They arrived after dinner and we felt like staying in, so Gracie and I gathered ingredients from my pantry and in just 15 minutes whipped together the most exceptional ginger molasses bread we've ever tasted.

8 tablespoons butter, softened, plus more for dish

2 teaspoons baking soda

2½ cups all-purpose flour, plus more for dish

2 tablespoons ground ginger

¾ teaspoon kosher salt

1 tablespoon baking powder

⅔ cup packed light brown sugar

1 cup unsulfured molasses

2 large eggs

confectioners' sugar, for serving

1. Preheat oven to 350 degrees. Lightly butter and flour a 4-quart temp-tations® dish. In a small bowl, microwave 1 cup water on high until boiling. Stir in the baking soda and set aside.

2. In a large bowl, whisk together the flour, ginger, salt, and baking powder.

3. In the bowl of a stand mixer fitted with a beater attachment, beat the butter and brown sugar on medium-high speed until light and fluffy, about 4 minutes. Beat in the molasses, baking soda, boiling water, and flour mixture. Beat in the eggs to combine. Pour the batter into the prepared dish.

4. Bake 45 minutes to 1 hour, or until a toothpick inserted in the center comes out clean. Transfer the ginger molasses bread to a wire rack to cool completely. Dust with confectioners' sugar, if desired.

TARA'S TRADITIONS *Caution!!! This bread can be addictive. Gracie loved it so much she asked Amy if she could have it for lunch as a sandwich with cream cheese in the middle and for dessert that night with whipped cream on top! That's my little Gracie! Hope she passes this on to her kids someday.*

DESSERTS

Baked Stuffed Apples

Simple and delicious. What a wonderful way to turn autumn fruit into a rich dessert. It's also a great way to make use of those apples that have been sitting in your fridge for too long.

¾ cups fresh bread crumbs, torn from day-old French bread (or white bread)

2 tablespoons packed light brown sugar

2 tablespoons golden raisins

3 tablespoons unsalted butter, melted

4 baking apples, such as Rome, Honeycrisp, Braeburn, or Gala

¼ cup apple cider or water

1. Preheat oven to 375 degrees.

2. In a medium bowl, mix the bread crumbs, brown sugar, raisins, and butter until combined.

3. Scoop out the core of each apple with a melon baller, being careful not to go through the bottom; discard cores.

4. Place the apples in a 2.5-quart temp-tations® dish and fill the holes with the bread-crumb mixture, tightly packing the filling. Pour cider into the bottom of the pan and cover the pan with foil.

5. Bake 30 minutes. Remove the foil and bake until apples are soft, but not mushy, and the crumb mixture is golden, 10 minutes more. Let cool slightly before serving.

TARA'S TRADITIONS *These apples are great with ham or pork, and I sometimes add some cream cheese and turn them into an entire meal. I like apple picking with my family, so I especially like making these in the fall.*

DESSERTS

Raspberry-Nilla Cheesecake Cupcakes

If you can't get this right, you need not be in the kitchen doing ANYTHING! Just kidding! The truth is, this was my first attempt at cheesecake and they were wonderful. I brought them to a Valentine's Day party and everyone thought that I had baked all day, but it took me less than an hour.

6 vanilla wafers

1 (8-ounce) package cream cheese, softened

⅓ cup plus 2 tablespoons white sugar, divided

1 egg

1 teaspoon vanilla extract

¼ cup sour cream

⅓ cup white chocolate, melted

2 teaspoons raspberry jam

6 frozen whole raspberries, defrosted

1 cup heavy cream

zest of one lemon

1. Preheat oven to 300 degrees. Line muffin pan with 6 paper baking cups. Place a vanilla wafer in each one.

2. In a medium mixing bowl, beat cream cheese until creamy and smooth. Add the sugar and mix until combined. Add the egg and mix until incorporated. Add the vanilla extract and sour cream and beat until incorporated.

3. In a separate bowl, mix white chocolate and raspberry jam.

4. Fill each baking cup with 1 tablespoon of the cream cheese mixture. Spoon 1 tablespoon of the white chocolate mixture in the center of every baking cup and top with another spoon of the cream cheese mixture.

5. Bake in preheated oven for 20 minutes. Cool on a rack.

6. Whip 1 cup heavy cream with 2 tablespoons sugar, and pipe it on top of the chilled cheesecake. Top each with a raspberry and lemon zest.

TARA'S TIDBITS™ *I doubled the recipe and baked half with cherry and half with blueberry. This recipe is quick, simple, and extremely easy to make. I've made this recipe several times over the past few weeks, opting for different variations of flavors. I made the crust with crushed graham crackers instead of vanilla wafers. I added white chocolate chips between the wafer and the filling. The opportunities are endless with this recipe!*

DESSERTS

PREP TIME: 15 mins   **COOK TIME: 30 mins**   **SERVES: 10 to 12**   **4 QUART**

Deana & Luna's Chocolate Tres Leches

LOVE this quick and easy super-moist recipe. They are so easy to make, my friend Deana's daughter, Luna, makes them for her mom all by herself (except for the oven and mixer, of course)! The kids always love to pitch in and help decorate this chocolate cake. It can serve a large party, or just my family…they always ask for seconds!

8 tablespoons unsalted butter, melted and cooled, plus more for dish

1¼ cups all-purpose flour

1 teaspoon baking powder

½ cup unsweetened cocoa, sifted

½ teaspoon Kosher salt

5 large eggs

¾ cup sugar

1 (14-ounce) can sweetened condensed milk

2 cups chocolate milk

2 cups heavy cream

chocolate sauce and chocolate curls, optional

1. Preheat oven to 350 degrees. Lightly butter a 4-quart rectangular temp-tations® dish. In a medium bowl, whisk together the flour, baking powder, cocoa, and salt.

2. In the bowl of a stand mixer fitted with the beater attachment, beat the eggs and ¾ cup sugar on high until thick, about 4 minutes. With mixer on low, gradually add the flour mixture and beat to combine. Gently fold in the melted butter until incorporated.

3. Transfer the batter to the prepared dish and bake 25 to 30 minutes or until a toothpick inserted in the center comes out clean.

4. In a medium bowl, whisk together the sweetened condensed milk and chocolate milk until combined. Poke the warm cake all over with a wooden skewer or toothpick and pour the milk mixture over top. Let cool to room temperature, about 1 hour.

5. Meanwhile, in the bowl of a stand mixer fitted with the whisk attachment, beat the cream on medium-high until soft peaks form, about 2 minutes. Top the cake with the whipped cream, chocolate sauce, and chocolate curls, if desired.

TARA'S TRADITIONS *Bring these to any potluck parties and be the first to come home with empty ovenware!*

Try drizzling chocolate sauce on top of this moist, dense cake.

DESSERTS

MORE HOT RECIPES IN COOL DISHES™ BY TARA®

Luna is my good friend Deana's daughter

and one of the most talented children I know. Luna draws like Picasso and cooks like Julia Child.

Chocolate Tres Leches is her mother's second favorite dessert (next to red velvet cupcakes) and that's what Luna likes to cook best. She always tells Mom that she's the best little baker in town. She always makes Mom meals like pizza with all the toppings and she loves to make "peanut butter, jelly, and sandwiches."

Luna always looks for Tara to bring her "smarshmellows" and they sneak them when Deana's not looking because Deana doesn't allow Luna to eat them!

She's in preschool, is four years old, loves to sing and dance and she's a little comedian. She has tons to say and talks from the minute she wakes up in the morning until she suddenly passes out at night. She is hilarious—the class clown. She's silly and loves to make people laugh with her amazing impressions.

Be on the lookout for Miss Luna in the near future. She's as gifted as she is nice as she is beautiful...just like her mother.

DESSERTS

MORE HOT RECIPES IN COOL DISHES™ BY TARA®

Dad was in the army when my parents got married and moved to the West Coast, away from their families. Mom was just seventeen and Dad was nineteen. Mom could just about make toast so she had to learn to cook from a book; it was that or literally starve. Mom always says, "If you can read, you can cook!" Well she is evidently a very good reader because she turned into quite an excellent cook. Nothing too fancy, most everything is made from everyday ingredients we either have in the pantry or are available almost anywhere. Mom worked when we were growing up, so her meals were fast and easy but they were always homemade. There was a meal on the table every night of the week. Mom returned home to ingredients already prepped by Dad, and her meals were ready to cook and serve in about thirty minutes. I remember that Sunday's leftovers also carried us through the week. As many of you know, my growing up in a family that brought people back to the table to create special memories and moments led me to design this line to transform the way we not only cook, but prepare, serve, reheat, store, and so much more! For more than eight years now, I've been blessed with sharing my designs and inspirations with all of you, and you've shared yours with me. We've become our own little family filled with pictures and moments of joy that we share with those closest to us—the family in our home.

Warmest Regards,

Tara

Tara McConnell, creator and designer of temp-tations® and author of Hot Recipes in Cool Dishes™ by Tara®, grew up in a small town one hour outside of New York City with her parents and sister. She's a graduate of West Virginia Wesleyan College.

In 2003, Tara brought her innovative concept of temp-tations® presentable ovenware™ to reality.

Tara's mom was her inspiration in bringing temp-tations® to you. Tara wanted her mom to be able to prepare their family meals ahead of time—and even freeze them—so their family would be able to have more time to visit with friends and relatives. Tara inherited her mom's love of cooking and hosting! With temp-tations® presentable ovenware™ Tara is not only able to plan ahead but also able to keep her oven and burners free, allowing her to prepare the rest of the dinner and do what she does best, entertain. She continues the legacy of her Mom.

In her free time (when she has any) Tara enjoys exercising, cooking, entertaining, spending time with family and friends, and giving back whenever she can.

MORE HOT RECIPES IN COOL DISHES™ BY TARA®

Acknowledgments

I want to thank everyone who has worked so tirelessly to help put this book together. I am surrounded by true talent and blessed to do something I love every day.

I want to thank Ed Tesher, Eric Levine, and Steve Giambruno for believing in me and temp-tations®—without them, none of this would be possible.

To my great temp-tations® and CSA work family...thank you for sharing in my vision and craziness. ☺

To my family—it's simple, I love you unconditionally with all my heart.

To the temp-tionistas (saved the best for last)—You fill me with inspiration and I enjoy every message, idea, and phone call that we share—thank you so very much for all the fun and good cooking!

❀ Tara

Recipe Index

Get recipes, ideas, and tips on mixing, matching, and collecting temp-tations® and talk to Tara and join others who have a passion for creating a beautiful presentation in the kitchen and on the table.

www.temp-tations.com